500 BEADED OBJECTS

Detail images from the works of
contributing artists (left to right):
Katherine Amacher Korff, Sage Zering,
Laura Willits, Jane Friedmann,
Marta Gilberd Sosna, Susan Etcoff Fraerman

5OO BEADED OBJECTS

New Dimensions in Contemporary Beadwork

LARK BOOKS

A Division of
Sterling Publishing Co., Inc.
New York

Library of Congress Cataloging-in-Publication Data

500 beaded objects : new dimensions in contemporary
beadwork / editor, Terry Krautwurst.-- 1st ed.
     p. cm.
 Includes index.
 ISBN 1-57990-549-8 (pbk.)
 1. Beadwork. 2. Beads. I. Krautwurst, Terry, 1946-
TT860.A17 2004
745.58'2--dc22
                                        2004001117

10 9 8 7 6 5 4 3 2 1

First Edition

Published by Lark Books, a division of
Sterling Publishing Co., Inc.
387 Park Avenue South, New York 10016

© 2004, Lark Books

Distributed in Canada by Sterling Publishing,
c/o Canadian Manda Group, One Atlantic Ave., Suite 105
Toronto, Ontario, Canada M6K 3E7

Distributed in the U.K. by Guild of Master Craftsman Publications Ltd.,
Castle Place, 166 High Street, Lewes, East Sussex, England
BN7 1XU
Tel: (+ 44) 1273 477374, Fax: (+ 44) 1273 478606,
Email: pubs@thegmcgroup.com, Web: www.gmcpublications.com

Distributed in Australia by Capricorn Link (Australia) Pty Ltd.,
P.O. Box 704, Windsor, NSW 2756 Australia

The works represented in this book are the original creations of the
contributing artists. All artists retain copyright on their individual works.

If you have questions or comments about this book, please contact:
Lark Books
67 Broadway
Asheville, NC 28801
(828) 253-0467

Manufactured in China

ISBN 1-57990-549-8

EDITOR: Terry Krautwurst
ART DIRECTOR: Kristi Pfeffer
COVER DESIGNER: Barbara Zaretsky
EDITORIAL ASSISTANCE: Delores Gosnell, Jeff Hamilton, Rosemary
Kast, Rebecca Guthrie, Nathalie Mornu
ASSOCIATE ART DIRECTORS: Lance Wille, Shannon Yokeley
EDITORIAL INTERNS: Meghan McGuire, Amanda Wheeler
ART INTERNS: Melanie Cooper, Jason Thompson

COVER IMAGES

Front, Robin Atkins, *Rosie the Uncaged Hen* (detail), 2001,
photo by Joe Manfredini

Back (clockwise from top left):
Madelyn C. Ricks, *Kimono*, 2000, photo by Jerry Anthony;
Ann Tevepaugh Mitchell, *Wading In*, 2003, photo by Dean
Powell; Valerie Hector, *Red Star Brooch—Parallels Series*,
2002, photo by Larry Sanders

Front flap, Jeanette Ahlgren, *Fighting Back the Gloom*, 2003,
photo by artist; back flap, Marcia Laging Cummings,
Lime/Orange, 2002, photo by Roger Bruhn; spine, Leslie
Ciechanowski, *World Fair*, 1998, photo by Larry Stessin

PAGE 1

Christmas Cowell, *If the Hat Fits...*, 2002,
photo by Tom Edelman

Contents

6
Introduction

8
THE BEADED OBJECTS

416
Acknowledgments

416
Artists

Introduction

When Lark Books called and asked if I would juror this book, I immediately said yes. What an honor to participate in a celebration of the pursuit I love, beading. But I confess that I was nervous about the responsibility. I hoped to select a diverse group of images, one that would represent the full spectrum of what is being done in the field today. I also hoped to include as many different artists as possible. But the jurying would be a blind process, meaning that I wouldn't know whose work I was viewing. Each creation had to speak for itself. Would the entries truly reflect the extraordinary course that beadwork is taking in our time?

You hold in your hands the resoundingly positive answer to that question. You are about to be amazed, as I am, by the seemingly limitless versatility of this medium: defined technically as anything with a hole in it, but mainly glass beads. You'll be amazed by the depth and breadth of technique represented here: embroidered, glued, handwoven using an off-loom stitch, strung, woven on a loom, combined with other media such as precious metals. Perhaps most of all, you'll be amazed by the divergent roads taken to create the vision only each artist sees.

Diversity of expression is communicated powerfully in this book by all 500 contemporary beaded objects and the wonderfully creative artists who made them. Witness, for example, Ann Tevepaugh Mitchell's *Wading In* (page 154), in which tiny glass beads become a woman standing by the seashore holding her sandals in her hands, her hair blowing in the breeze, dipping her toes into the surf.

Both Jacqueline I. Lillie and Sharon M. Donovan have combined the art of beading with the art of metalsmithing, but each evokes a distinctly personal style, a unique feeling within her work. Jacqueline's pieces (pages 32, 46, 142, 311) have an air of crisp sophistication and Sharon's work (pages 10, 11, 143, 303, 309) moves us through times past and into the future.

Kim Z Franklin puts her use of metal and beads on the wall with *Blind Obedience* (page 73), a striking image portraying the opening of "our" eyes to see what is beyond the obvious—there is always more if we could only see!

Bonnie A. Berkowitz uses the art form as a way to tell a story—the meaning is hidden within the framework of the piece. *Mother May I: Accordion Book Bra* (page 55) and *The Levite's Daughter: A Sole Book* (page 297) take utilitarian objects and spin our desires and memories into bead-encrusted works of art.

Detail images from the works of contributing artists (left to right): Ronnie Lambrou, Jan Zicarelli, Leslie Ciechanowski, Joanne Strehle Bast, Marcie Stone, SaraBeth Cullinan

Stories can be told through sculpture as well. Each of A.Kimberlin Blackburn's dimensional pieces (pages 129, 156, 207, 350) draws us into the tropical beaded fantasy that is her creative vision. These works are strong, bold, and full, taking the viewer into an island paradise.

Not all images lead us directly into the thoughts of the artist, but upon reading the title of the work we can immediately go there. A visual verbal construct tells all in Natasha St. Michael's works: *Infested* (page 144), *Ferment* (page 145), *Spindle* (page 231), and *Porous* (page 267).

Linda Fifield also uses this type of communication within the form of her vessels. Looking at *Fire on the Mountain* and *Earth Ablaze* (page 37), one can almost feel the heat and sense the beauty that is fire.

Beadwork is a time-consuming labor of love. A 1-inch square of peyote stitch using 11° seed beads can take 30 minutes to make and requires 220 beads, picked up one at a time. Now consider a piece 10 x 12 inches, or 120 square inches. At 220 beads and half an hour per square inch, that's 26,400 beads and 60 hours to make. And that's just plain peyote stitch; add in a pattern and the time is doubled.

So why do it? Why spend all of those hours picking up beads one by one with a needle while hunched over a table or desk? The answer lies somewhere in the tactile and scintillating quality of beads and in the heart of the artist, who uses her hands to capture a moment of personal meaning and then passes that moment on to the viewer.

Beads are at once singular and lively; in the joining, they gain luminosity and grace, while taking the artist along for the ride. Whether the work is free-form or planned, each time a bead is about to be picked up and added to the work in progress, the artist has to choose which bead to use. Which type of bead would work best? Which color will enhance the beads around it? What size bead should be used? As a piece of beadwork is coming to form, the mind is looking forward and backward, seeing the relationships to come and the ones already made. It is a constant, quiet working meditation—one that lets the hours pass unawares, a joyful time of creation.

500 Beaded Objects is a stunning celebration of what a seemingly humble medium can become in the hands and hearts of artists, each with a different perspective on the use of beads as a means of expression. As you look at this body of work, marvel, with me, at the diversity of what is being done in this field today. It is indeed a time of wonder for creative achievement in beadwork.

Carol Wilcox Wells

The Beaded Objects

TERRY PYLES
Gila Monster, 2003

8½ x 3½ x 1½ in. (21.6 x 8.9 x 3.8 cm)
Seed beads, modeling compound; peyote stitch
Photo by Joe Manfredini

In real life the gila monster looks like it's beaded, so I thought it would be fun to imitate life with beads.

This was inspired by a Japanese story about a boy who painted cats on screens. The cats were so realistic that they came alive and saved his life.

JUDY WALKER
The Boy Who Painted Cats, 1999

16 x 24 x 10 in. (40.6 x 61 x 25.4 cm)
Cylinder seed beads, bone dagger beads, glass taxidermy
eyes, shed cat whiskers; loom woven, peyote stitch
Photo by Richard Walker

9

SHARON M. DONOVAN
Treasure House Bracelet, 2002

1¾ x 7½ in. (4.4 x 19 cm)
Sterling silver, gold, seed beads; fabricated, strung
Photo by Larry Sanders

*Inspired by a 1,000-year-old
Japanese lantern.*

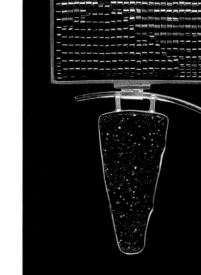

CAROL WILCOX WELLS
*In All of My Travels the Root
of My Being Lives Here*, 2003

2¾ x 1⅞ in. (6.9 x 4.8 cm)
Cylinder seed beads, druzy, sterling silver;
fabricated, layered square stich
Photo by Tim Barnwell

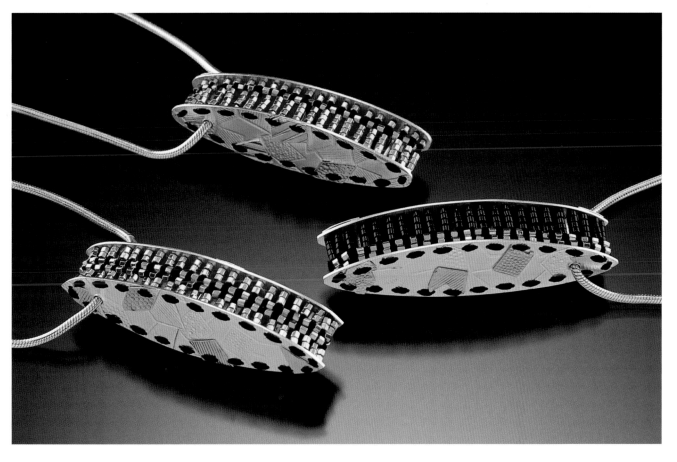

The thread for these pieces is woven through the beads twice.

SHARON M. DONOVAN
Beaded Pods I, II & III, 2003

3 x ½ x ¾ in. (7.6 x 1.3 x 1.9 cm)
Sterling silver, gold, cylinder seed beads; fabricated, woven
Photo by Larry Sanders

JEAN CAMPBELL
Did You Ever See Such a Sight ..., 2001

8 x 5 in. (20.3 x 12.7 cm)
Seed beads, pressed glass beads, aluminum, wire; sculptural peyote stitch, wirework
Photo by Joe Coca

This formidable farmer's wife will make quick work of those mouse tails. (Why does everyone say this is a self-portrait?)

CHARLOTTE R. MILLER
Two to Tango, 2002

9¾ x 4½ x¾ in. (24.7 x 11.4 x 1.9 cm)
Seed beads, pony beads, sterling silver wire; wirework
Photo by Bill LaMond

*I was inspired to re-create the beauty
and sensuality of the tango after watching
a performance of the dance. One hundred
hours later, Two to Tango was born.*

ANN TEVEPAUGH MITCHELL
The Birdwatcher, 2000

15 x 8 x 6 in. (38.1 x 20.3 x 15.2 cm)
Glass beads, glass, stones; peyote stitch, assembled improvisationally
Photo by Dean Powell
Collection of Dr. Gary Wetreich

13

CHRIS ANN PHILIPS
God Bless the King, 2002

5¾ x 4¾ x 2 in. (14.6 x 12 x 5 cm)
Seed beads, assorted beads and accents,
ceramic face by Michael Barnes; peyote stitch,
right-angle weave, bead embroidery
Photo by Mark Dressler

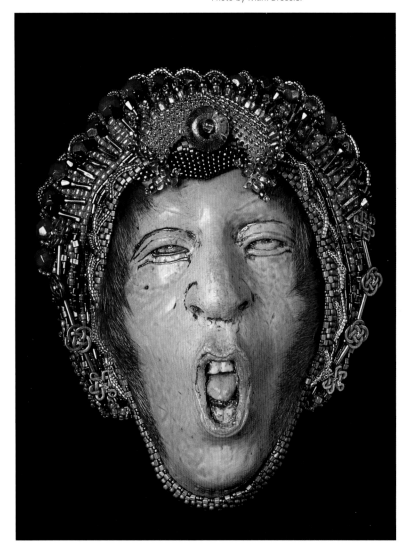

*When I started
working on this
face, I called him*
The Very Rude Man.
*As I embellished him,
he evolved to look
like he's sneezing.*

WENDY SEAWARD
Wild Woman in Green, 2000

9 x 12 in. (22.9 x 30.5 cm)
Seed beads, found object, cast armature,
felt backing; peyote stitch
Photo by Robert Batey

ELEANOR LUX
Baby Ball, 2002

9 x 9 x 9 in. (22.9 x 22.9 x 22.9 cm)
Seed beads, fabric-covered gourd,
found doll parts; beads couched
onto gourd
Photo by Cindy Momchilou

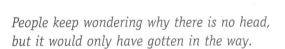

*People keep wondering why there is no head,
but it would only have gotten in the way.*

DAVID K. CHATT
Flab Bag, 2000

8 x 10 x 8 in. (20.3 x 25.4 x 20.3 cm)
Assorted glass beads, glass marbles; right-angle weave
Photo by Harriet Burger
Collection of Bill Shelby and Alison Gardner Shelby

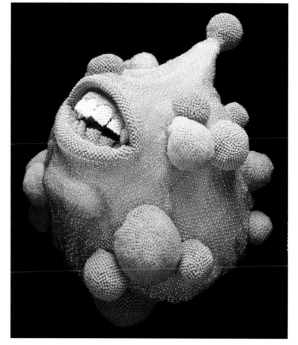

SONYA Y. S. CLARK
Blued, 1998

10 x 15 x 8 in. (25.4 x 38.1 x 20.3 cm)
Seed beads; peyote stitch
Photo by Tom McInvaille
Collection of Darryl Harper

17

AL KRUEGER
Good Boy, 2003

24 x 32 in. (61 x 81.3 cm)
Seed beads, assorted beads, vintage pillowcase;
bead embroidery, Ndebele stitch, peyote stitch
Photo by Tom Van Eynde

This is a self-portrait using my high school graduation picture, circa 1967.

VIRGINIA BRUBAKER
Woman Musing, 2002

4¾ x 4½ x 1¾ in. (12 x 11.4 x 4.4 cm)
Seed beads, wood support; brick stitch
Photo by artist

VIRGINIA BRUBAKER
Self-Portrait in Blue, 2003

8¼ x 6¼ in. (21 x 15.8 cm)
Seed beads; bead embroidery
Photo by artist

19

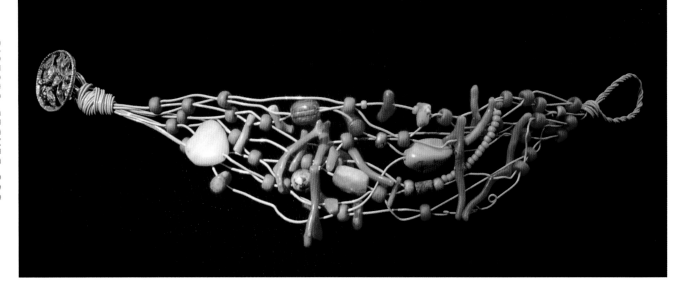

LEA WORCESTER
Charlotte's Web Bracelet Branching Out, 2003

7½ x 2½ in. (19 x 6.4 cm)
Turquoise, aventurine, African trade beads, antique coral,
antique button; free-form weave
Photo by Ruby Jewel

VALERIE HECTOR
Red Star Brooch—Parallels Series, 2002

3¾ x 3¾ x ½ in. (9.5 x 9.5 x 1.3 cm)
Cylindrical seed beads, hex-cut metal beads, silver
armature; peyote stitch tubes around armature
Photo by Larry Sanders
Private collection

My Parallels *series brooches are inspired by seventeenth-century embroidered wickerwork shields from the Ottoman Empire.*

TOM WEGMAN
Beaded Fan, 2003

14 x 11 x 7 in.
(35.6 x 27.9 x 17.8 cm)
Seed beads, rhinestone
jewelry and chain,
vintage fan; glued
Photo by David Trawick

21

*Warm nights,
sweet flowers,
lush lawns,
everyone dancing
in the moonlight
till dawn.
Wouldn't you
delight to wear
a pair to a garden
party tonight?*

DIANN M. COTTRILL
Garden Party Shoe, 2000

6 x 4½ x 8½ in. (15.2 x 11.4 x 21.6 cm)
Seed beads, bugles, flower and butterfly beads,
crystal, wire, suedelike fabric; peyote stitch,
right-angle weave, other stitches
Photo by Randy Hoover Photography

22

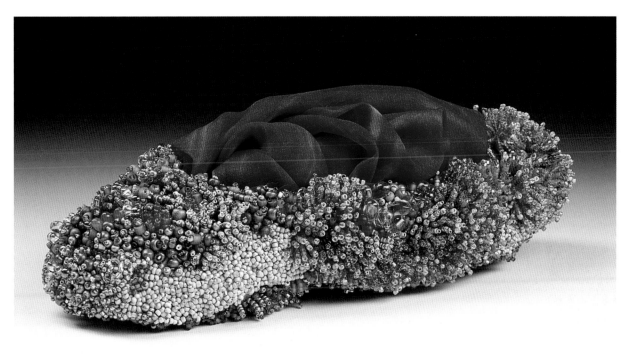

SUSAN ETCOFF FRAERMAN
One Soul: Shoe Number Fourteen, 2001

4 x 9 x 3½ in. (10.2 x 22.9 x 8.9 cm)
Seed beads, other glass beads, leather,
artist-dyed silk organza; off-loom bead weaving,
free-form right-angle weave
Photo by Tom Van Eynde

MICHELLE WILLIAMS
Sabotaging the Working Lady, 1996

7 x 7 x 6½ in. (17.8 x 17.8 x 16.5 cm)
Seed beads, assorted beads, quartz crystal, cotton, suede;
peyote stitch, fringe, stitching, spikes
Photo by Wilmer Zehr
Collection of Ricki Angelus

This piece represents the process of overcoming obstacles,
and my success in turning a negative situation into a positive one.

SHERRY MARKOVITZ
Steel Prayer, 2001–2003

12 x 11 x 6 in. (30.5 x 27.9 x 15.2 cm)
Papier-mâché, steel-cut beads; peyote stitch, bead embroidery
Photo by artist
Courtesy of Greg Kucera Gallery

This piece followed a series of paintings concerning 9/11. After finishing those pieces, I felt that prayer was all that was left. I like the fact that the steel-cut beads were once German bullets that were used to make beaded purses, and now are in my work. After 25 years of working with beads, I've come to love the colors of the old ones.

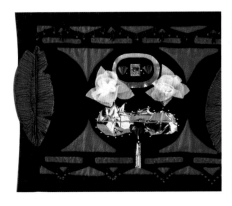

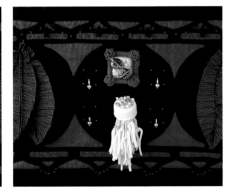

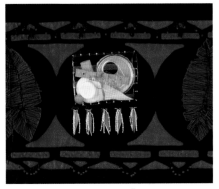
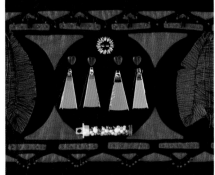

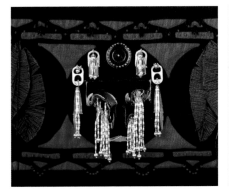

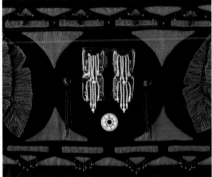

ROBINSUNNE
I Will Embroider My Grief, 2002

10 x 140 x 1 in. (25.4 x 355.6 x 2.5 cm)
Seed beads, pony beads, bugles,
sterling silver beads, pearls, coins,
plastic, metal, foam, card, shell, other
found objects, polymer clay, cotton
broadcloth; appliqué, machine- and
hand-sewn, strung, manipulated,
embellished
Photo by William Thuss

I took my grief to my studio, and this is what happened.
The piece is a bit more than 11 feet (3.4 m) long with 13
panels of appliquéd cloth. I worked early each morning for a
couple of hours before my young children awoke, and five
months later, when I set my needle down, I knew that it is
true what they say: Art saves lives.

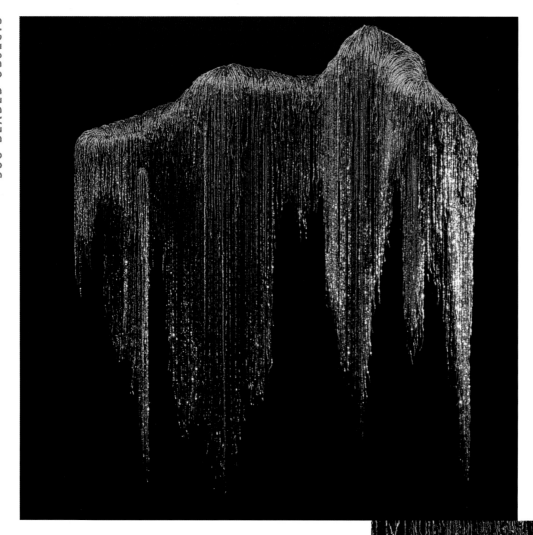

JAMES EDWARD TALBOT
Benediction, 2003

30 x 27 x 13 in. (76.2 x 68.5 x 33 cm)
Seed beads, yarn-wrapped steel armature; wrapped, fringe
Photo by Catherine McMillan

CINDY WROBEL
Homage to a Tree I, 2001

21 x 8½ x 3½ in. (53.3 x 21.6 x 8.9 cm)
Seed beads, assorted beads, rock, wire; strung on wire,
wrapped around wire framework
Photo by Jim Sokolik

CINDY WROBEL
Siren of the Sea, 2003

18 x 9 x 13 in. (45.7 x 22.9 x 33 cm)
Assorted beads, wire, wood, found objects, printed tin; strung on
wire, wrapped around wire framework and carved wood form
Photo by Jim Sokolik

FRAN MENELEY
Lasirena, 2003

11½ x 8½ x 2 in. (29.2 x 21.6 x 5 cm)
Seed beads, vintage sequins, assorted vintage
and new beads, silk, miniature shoes, seashells,
altered book, stone base
Photo by Robert Morrissey

31

DONNA ZAIDENBERG
No Connections, 2003

9 x ¾ in. (22.9 x 1.9 cm)
Seed beads, cylinder seed beads,
freshwater pearls; tubular Ndebele stitch
Photo by Jim DeWayne

*I wanted to make a
bracelet that would stay
in place without any closure,
and that was sophisticated
but not fussy.*

JACQUELINE I. LILLIE
Three Magnetic Brooches, 2000

1½ to 2½ in. (3.8 to 6.4 cm)
Antique glass and metal beads, silver mounting,
magnetic clasps; individually knotted
Photo by Kohl and Oláh
Courtesy of Rosanne Raab Associates

JENNIFER MOKREN
Dotted Vessel #2, 2003

3 x 4 x 4 in. (7.6 x 10.2 x 10.2 cm)
Cylinder seed beads, sterling silver;
peyote stitch, fabricated silver elements
Photo unattributed

CHRISTINE MARIE NOGUERE
Aphrodite's Secret, 2003

2½ x 2½ x 2 in. (6.4 x 6.4 x 5 cm)
Seed beads, cylinder seed beads, brass,
suedelike fabric, rubber rings, freshwater
pearls; peyote stitch, right-angle weave,
pearls sewn (not glued)
Photo by Phil Pope

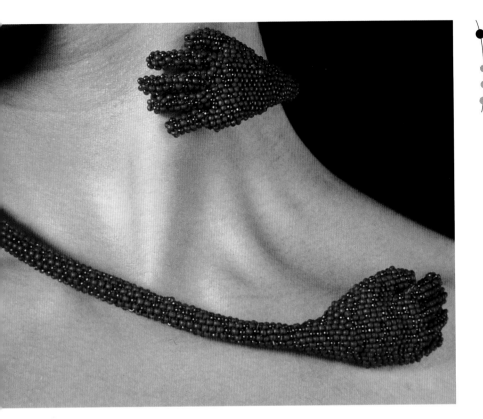

SONYA Y. S. CLARK
Little Hug, 2002

3 x 5 x 5 in. (7.6 x 12.7 x 12.7 cm)
Seed beads; peyote stitch
Photo by Tom McInvaille

SONYA Y. S. CLARK
Inner Hand, 2001

1 x 5 x 2 in. (2.5 x 12.7 x 5 cm)
Seed beads; peyote stitch
Photo by Tom McInvaille
Collection of James Dozier

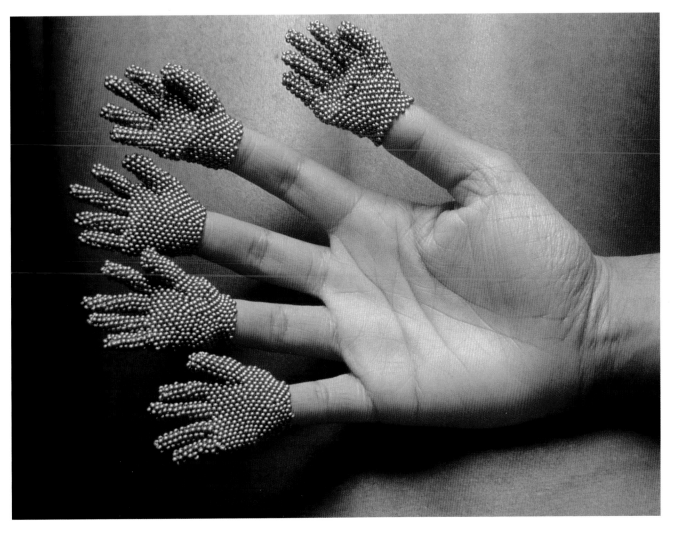

SONYA Y. S. CLARK
Golden Touch, 2002

Each, 1 x ½ x ½ in. (2.5 x 1.3 x 1.3 cm)
Seed beads; peyote stitch
Photo by Tom McInvaille

KATHY SEELY
Plays Well with Fire, 2001

16 in. (40.6 cm)
Seed beads, vintage glass beads, black onyx, cylinder seed
beads; variation of peyote stitch
Photo by Robert Batey

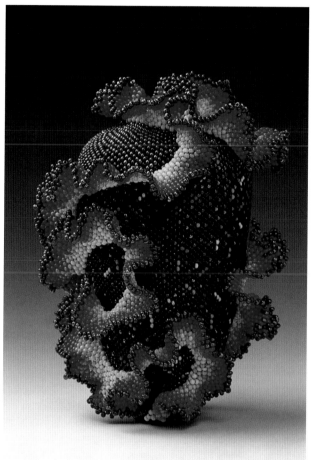

LINDA FIFIELD
Earth Ablaze, 2002

6 x 4 x 4 in. (15.2 x 10.2 x 10.2 cm)
Seed beads, turned wooden vessel;
gourd stitch
Photo by Jack Fifield

LINDA FIFIELD
Fire on the Mountain, 2002

7 x 4 x 4 in. (17.8 x 10.2 x 10.2 cm)
Seed beads, turned wooden vessel;
gourd stitch
Photo by Jack Fifield

37

ANA M. GARCIA
Ablaze, 2001

16 x 2 in. (40.6 x 5 cm)
Seed beads; right-angle weave, fringe
Photo by Melinda Holden

My interest here is creating a sense of weightlessness and luminescence by the manipulation of industrial wire and glass beads.

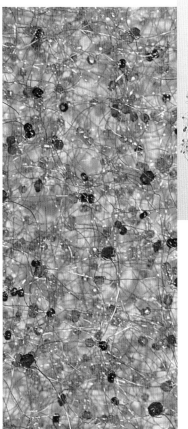

NANCY KOENIGSBERG
Radiant, 1999

33 x 33 x 4 in. (83.8 x 83.8 x 10.2 cm)
Glass beads lined with gold foil, assorted
gold glass beads, coated copper wire;
square-knotted with beads incorporated in
each knot, about 10 layers of beaded nets
Photo by D. James Dee
Private collection

39

MARGO C. FIELD
Bakelite and Trumpet Vine, 2000

14 x 8 x 1½ in. (35.6 x 20.3 x 3.8 cm)
Seed beads, assorted beads, vintage glass pearls,
Bakelite pieces; peyote stitch, branched fringe
Photo by Pat Berrett
Detail photo by Karen Neisany

*The Bakelite pieces clearly said
to me that they were leaves,
and insisted that they needed
orange-red flowers to be complete!*

SUZANNE DICKERSON
Mistress of the Jungle, 2003

8½ x 6 x 1 in. (21.6 x 15.2 x 2.5 cm)
Seed beads, crystals, Swarovski crystals,
carved tagua nut, memory wire; sculptural
peyote stitch, brick stitch
Photo by Mark R. Swindler
Artist's collection

KATHY SEELY
Summer Forest, 1999

16 x 6 x 1 in. (40.6 x 15.2 x 2.5 cm)
Cylinder seed beads, seed beads,
carved wood clasp, rayon cord;
peyote stitch, brick stitch,
sculptural variations
Photo by Robert Batey

*I challenged myself to
create accurate leaf shades
and colors using only
small beads and sculptural
stitching techniques,
some of which were
invented on the fly.*

HUIB PETERSEN
Circle of Life, 2001

1 x 4 x 23 in.
(2.5 x 10.2 x 58.4 cm)
Seed beads, pearls;
peyote stitch,
herringbone stitch
Photo by George Post
Collection of J. P. Tupper

MARCIE STONE
Reef Walker, 1999

6¾ x 10 x 4½ in. (17.1 x 25.4 x 11.4 cm)
Modern and antique seed beads, turquoise, coral and antique
beads, thermoplastic armature; sculptural peyote stitch
Photo by Melinda Holden

WENDY ELLSWORTH
"Tongatapu" Sea Form, 2001

4 3/4 x 5 x 5 in. (12 x 12.7 x 12.7 cm)
Seed beads, glass lentil beads, daggers;
free-form herringbone stitch, gourd stitch
Photo by David Ellsworth

*My husband's scuba
diving trips take us
to many tropical
destinations. My need
to interpret the beauty
around me, and the
sights my husband
sees while diving,
drove me to create
this colorful work.*

JO ANN BAUMANN
Memories of Mexico, 1999

5 x 5 x 3 in. (12.7 x 12.7 x 7.6 cm)
Seed beads, assorted beads, antique sequins,
cloth, polyester fiberfill; flat and three-dimensional
bead embroidery
Photo by Tom Van Eynde

JACQUELINE I. LILLIE
Earclips, 2000

1 x 1 in. (2.5 x 2.6 cm)
Antique glass beads, aluminum,
stainless steel spring; individually knotted
Photo by Kohl and Oláh
Courtesy of Rosanne Raab Associates

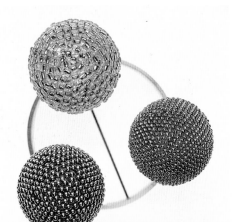

AXEL RUSSMEYER
BrOOOch!, 2001

1¼ x 2 x 2 in. (3.2 x 5 x 5 cm)
Antique aluminum beads, vintage metallic
glass beads, vintage gold-lined glass beads,
acrylic spheres, steel wire, yellow gold
Photo by Geoff Onyett

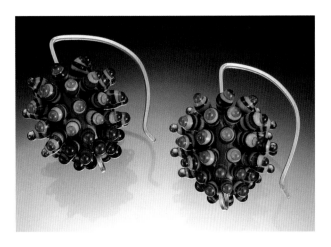

KATE ROTHRA
Bromeliad Earrings, 2003

1 in. (2.5 cm)
Handblown lampworked glass beads, sterling silver
Photo by Ralph Gabriner

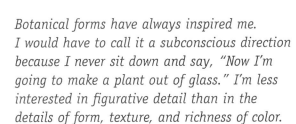

*Botanical forms have always inspired me.
I would have to call it a subconscious direction
because I never sit down and say, "Now I'm
going to make a plant out of glass." I'm less
interested in figurative detail than in the
details of form, texture, and richness of color.*

ELEANORE MACNISH
"Casino" Series Collar Necklace, 2002

Necklace, 20 x 2 x ¼ in. (50.8 x 5 x .6 cm)
Soda-lime glass beads, sterling silver,
glass beads made by artist; wirework
Photo by David Nufer
Private collection

*I was standing at a blackjack table in
a casino and noticed how all of the chips
looked spread out on the table.
"What a wonderful bead design,"
I thought.*

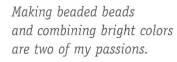

JO ANN BAUMANN
Bodacious Beaded Beads, 2003

9 x 8 x 1¼ in. (22.9 x 20.3 x 3.2 cm)
Seed beads, assorted beads, clear acrylic
balls; right-angle weave
Photo by Larry Sanders

*Making beaded beads
and combining bright colors
are two of my passions.*

47

YOSHIE MARUBASHI
One Sunny Day, 2001

10 in. (25.4 cm)
Seed beads, assorted beads,
buttons, canvas shoes; bead
embroidery, netting, crochet
Photo by artist

*This project took me
four months to complete.*

TOM WEGMAN
Babe Rainbow Skates, 2003

9 x 11 x 4½ in.
(22.9 x 27.9 x 11.4 cm)
Seed beads, roller skates;
glued, strung
Photo by David Trawick

DUSTIN WEDEKIND
Labyrinth Sandals, 2000

11 x 4 x 2 in. (27.9 x 10.2 x 5 cm)
Seed beads, felt; bead embroidery
Photo by Joe Coca

*One sandal shows Theseus
with his golden thread;
the other shows the Minotaur
that waits for him at the
center of the Labyrinth.*

DUSTIN WEDEKIND
Icarus, 2003

12 x 3 in. (30.5 x 7.6 cm)
Seed beads, sequins, tie; bead embroidery
Photo by Reeds Photo Imaging

DUSTIN WEDEKIND
Temperance, 2002

12 x 3½ in. (30.5 x 8.9 cm)
Seed beads, sequins, tie; bead embroidery
Photo by Reeds Photo Imaging

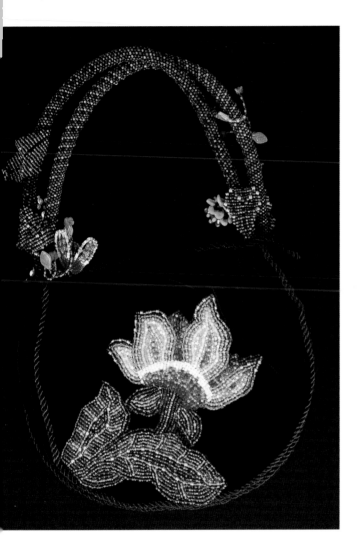

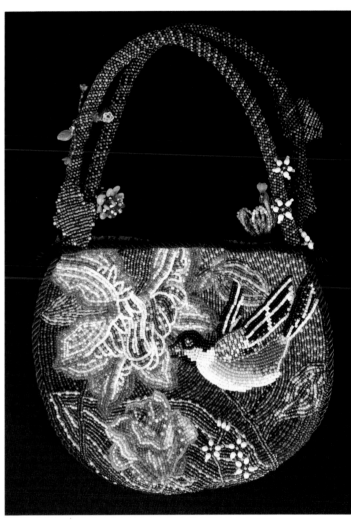

KATHLYN LEIGHTON
Celebrate Spring, 2002

12 x 8 x 1 in. (30.5 x 20.3 x 2.5 cm)
Seed beads, two-cut and cylinder seed beads, small pearls;
bead embroidery, tubular peyote stitch, square stitch
Photo by Durk Park

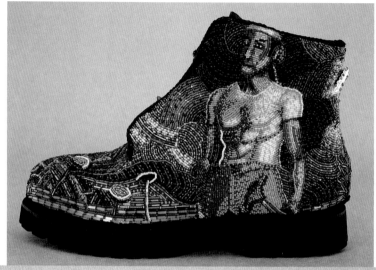

KATHLYN LEIGHTON
Hardworking Man, 2002

8¼ x 5 x 12½ in. (20.9 x 12.7 x 31.8 cm)
Seed beads, bugles, two-cuts, cylinder seed
beads, sequins, wire; bead embroidery
Photo by Durk Park

VALORIE HARLOW
Toe Mangler, 2000

6 x 6 x 18 in. (15.2 x 15.2 x 45.7 cm)
Seed beads, assorted beads; right-angle weave, peyote stitch
Photo by Petronella Ytsma

This piece is about women wearing
uncomfortable shoes and what we do
to ourselves in the name of fashion.

CINDY WROBEL
Beauty Within, Beauty Without—Bustier, 2002

9 x 9 x 7½ in. (22.9 x 22.9 x 19 cm)
Assorted beads, pearls, garnet, wire, found objects;
strung on wire, wrapped around wire framework
Photo by Jim Sokolik

*The title words beaded in
the vertical panels remind us
of the two sides of beauty.*

BONNIE A. BERKOWITZ
Mother May I: Accordion Book Bra, 2000

12 x 10½ x 8 in. (30.5 x 26.7 x 20.3 cm)
Glass beads, damask, antique fabric, wire, muslin, red cotton,
metallic threads, cathedral beads, bra; bead embroidery
Photo by Peter Jacobs
Collection of A. Kardon

*From each nipple, a fabric accordion book
can be gently pulled to reveal a message
about feeling capable to express oneself.*

JO WOOD
Moose Maple, 2003

9½ x 9¼ x ⅜ in. (24.1 x 23.5 x .95 cm)
Seed beads, wool yarn, felted wool; bead embroidery
Photo by Steven M. Tiggemann, Jeff Frey & Associates

The turning of the moose maple marks the first bold stroke of autumn's flaming palette against summer's green.

JAN ZICARELLI
Orange Bowl, 1997

2½ x 7 x 7 in. (6.4 x 17.8 x 17.8 cm)
Seed beads, semiprecious stone chips,
assorted glass beads, cotton yarn;
bead crochet, fringe
Photo by Peter Lee

MADELYN C. RICKS
Late Bloomer, 1999

14 x 7 x 16 in. (35.6 x 17.8 x 40.6 cm)
Cylinder seed beads; peyote stitch
Photo by Jerry Anthony

*The leaves aren't attached;
they just wrap around the stem.
I chose the name of the piece
because I didn't start beading
until late in life.*

57

ADELE RECKLIES
The Twins: 2 Green Snakes, 1999–2000

34 x 1 x ¾ in. (86.3 x 2.5 x 1.9 cm)
Seed beads, cotton; crochet
Photo by Donald Recklies

Each snake can be worn as a necklace by threading the tail through the mouth.

NanC MEINHARDT
Sssssssnake, 2000

10 x 8 x 4 in. (25.4 x 20.3 x 10.2 cm)
Seed beads, assorted beads, wire mesh; applied beads
Photo by Tom Van Eynde
Collection of Larry and Rita Sibrack

This piece can be worn several ways. Jacks cubes are also intended to be used as game pieces—with a gilded rubber ball—to play my favorite childhood game, jacks.

PENNY HARRELL
Jacks Cubes Necklace, 1999

16 in. (40.6 cm)
Glass beads, semiprecious chips; right-angle weave
Photo by Hap Sakwa

60

NORMA SHAPIRO
Untitled, 2002

27 in. (68.6 cm)
Seed beads, lampworked glass bead
and clasp, gold rings, copper cones;
kumihimo braiding, square stitch
Photo by artist

*Kumihimo braiding is
traditionally done with
silk threads but may also
be done with beads or a
combination of beads
and threads.*

JÓH RICCI
Four Seasons, 2001

16 in. (40.6 cm)
Cylinder seed beads, Czech glass; crochet
Photo by Norman Watkins

SCOTT SCHULDT
Initiation: The Patriarch, 2003

17 x 10 x 5 in. (43.2 x 25.4 x 12.7 cm)
Modern and vintage seed beads,
fully functional backpack made of deer
hide and nylon by artist; lane stitch,
overlay stitch
Photo by artist

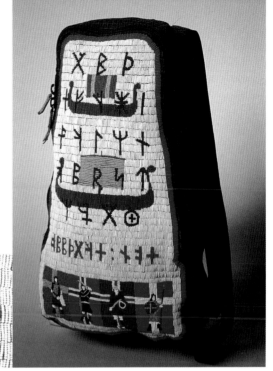

SCOTT SCHULDT
Oppdag Noe, 2001

17 x 10 x 5 in. (43.2 x 25.4 x 12.7 cm)
Modern and vintage seed beads, fully functional backpack made
of nylon by artist; lane stitch, overlay stitch
Photo by artist

*This piece is a sampler of a thirteenth-century
runic alphabet, Futhark, shown in the order
of the modern English alphabet.*

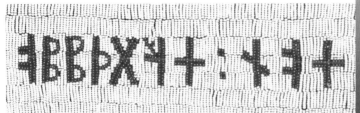

SCOTT SCHULDT
Sydpolsekk, 2001

17 x 10 x 5 in. (43.2 x 25.4 x 12.7 cm)
Modern and vintage seed beads, fully functional backpack made
of nylon by artist; lane stitch, overlay stitch, crow stitch
Photo by artist

*Sydpolsekk is Norwegian for "South Pole pack."
This work shows the Norwegian team led by
Roald Amundsen shortly after reaching the South
Pole in 1911.*

JENNIFER GALLAGHER
Fantasy Duck, 2001

Duck, 5 x 2¾ x 5 in. (13 x 7 x 13 cm);
walking stick, 51½ in. (130.8 cm)
Seed beads, faceted glass beads,
oak walking stick by Karl H. Reuss;
peyote stitch, right-angle weave, fringe
Photo by Andrew Lundgren

JENNIFER GALLAGHER
Ducktude, 2000

Duck, 6½ x 4 x 5½ in. (17 x 10 x 14 cm);
walking stick, 53½ in. (135.9 cm)
Seed beads, pressed glass beads, pearls,
bugles, oak walking stick by Karl H. Reuss;
peyote stitch, right-angle weave
Photo by Andrew Lundgren

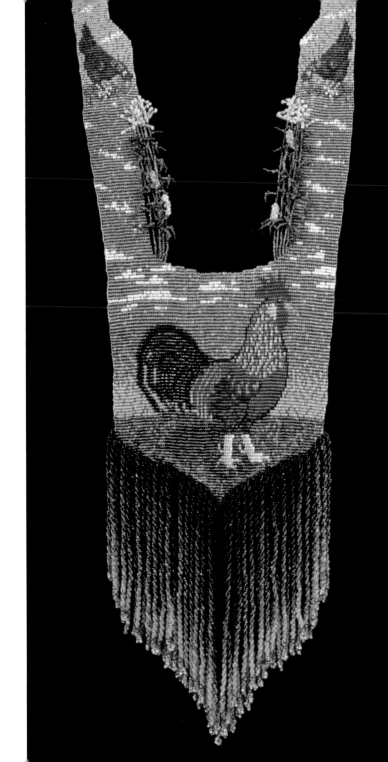

CAROL PERRENOUD
Chauntecler of Cockaigne, 1994

17 x 3¼ x ⅛ in. (43.2 x 8.2 x .3 cm)
Vintage seed beads; loom woven,
twisted fringe
Photo by artist

OLGA DVIGOUBSKY CINNAMON
Guarded Optimism, 2003

13 x 7 x 1½ in. (33 x 17.8 x 3.8 cm)
Assorted glass beads, sterling silver,
metal washers, nuts and bolts, fabric stuffing;
crochet, free-form beadwork
Photo by Jeff Owen

MARY H. KARG
Guardian Spirit XVI—Diviner, 2003

12 x 3 x 2 in. (30.5 x 7.6 x 5 cm)
Handmade lampworked glass beads
(head, stand, bird, and basket), bear claws,
vintage feathers, seed beads, fossilized
tree coral, mahogany, shells; branch stitch
Photo by Jerry Anthony Photography

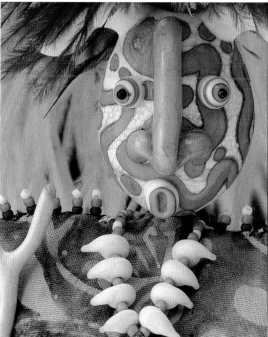

*This particular guardian
spirit was inspired by
the basket diviners of
Angola's Chokwe people.*

JENNIFER WHITTEN
Ancestral Being, 2002

9½ x 6 in. (24.1 x 15.2 cm)
Seed beads, vintage sequins, felt, fabric, embroidery floss,
glass; bead embroidery, glass fusing
Photo by CLIX

This was inspired by images found in the cave markings of aboriginal cultures.

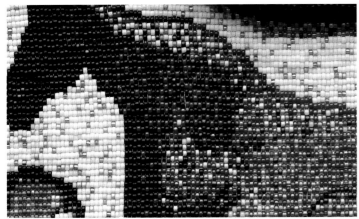

BARBARA BERG
Lascaux Collar, 2002

20½ x 15½ x 5 in. (52 x 39.4 x 12.7 cm)
Seed beads; loom woven, tubular peyote stitch
Photo by D. James Dee

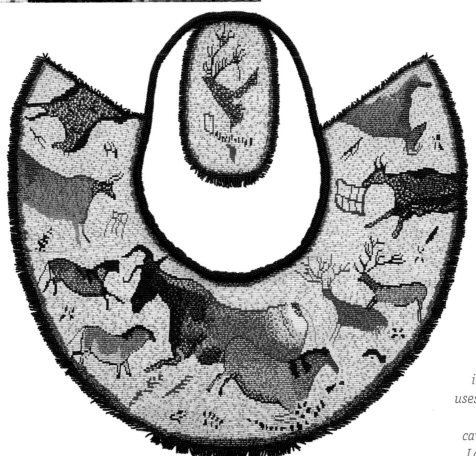

This piece is inspired by and uses imagery from the prehistoric cave paintings in Lascaux, France.

69

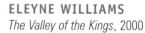

ELEYNE WILLIAMS
The Valley of the Kings, 2000

29 x 18 in. (73.6 x 45.7 cm)
Seed beads, other beads (including brass,
faience, clay, bone, bugles, glass), lapis lazuli,
carnelian, carved and painted wooden barge;
loom and off-loom woven
Photo by Kit Williams
Private collection of Ray and Diana Hayward

DENEEN MATSON
Forever Beading III, 2001

18 x 16 x 1 in. (45.7 x 40.6 x 2.5 cm)
Matted seed beads, assorted beads;
peyote stitch, brick stitch
Photo by Tom Van Eynde

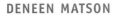

SHARMINI WIRASEKARA
Tlingit Man's Shirt, 2002

9 x 10 x 1 in. (22.9 x 25.4 x 2.5 cm)
Cylinder seed beads, acrylic fur trim, black cotton fabric,
clear acrylic stand; peyote stitch
Photo by Ros Aylmer

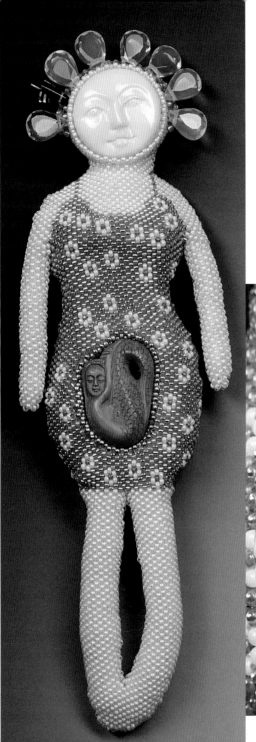

SHEREE WILCOX
Nurture Doll, 2003

7¼ x 2⅓ x ¾ in. (18.4 x 6 x 1.9 cm)
Seed beads, assorted glass beads, carved bone face; peyote stitch
Photo by Tom Van Eynde

Here I portrayed a modern girl/woman pregnant. She wears a sweet albeit sexy lavender dress; her tiara gives her an angelic bent, offsetting the dress. Her face is pure and virginlike.

KIM Z FRANKLIN
Blind Obedience, 2002

48 x 54 x 10 in. (122 x 137.2 x 25.4 cm)
Seed beads, hand-formed clay understructure, hand-forged metal
framework by artist and Michael Franklin; sculptural peyote stitch
Photo by Donna Chiarelli

To follow blindly is to deny personal growth.
We should consider ourselves lucky if at some
point in our life our preconceived ideas are
challenged and our eyes are made to open.
This was the inspiration for this piece.

73

DON PIERCE
Art Deco #7, 2002

20 x 6 in. (50.8 x 15.2 cm)
Cylinder seed beads, gold clasp; loom woven
Photo by Martin Kilmer

BETSEY-ROSE WEISS
Nipple Necklace, 1992–1993

6 x 6½ x ⅜ in. (15.2 x 16.5 x .9 cm)
Seed beads, pony beads, felt, leather;
bead embroidery, knotting, stitching
Photo by Will Crocker
Collection of April Bress

BETTE KELLEY
Amulet, 1993–1994

15 x 5½ in. (38.1 x 14 cm)
Bugle beads, faience beads, money tusks, dentalium shells, coral, steatite scarab, seed beads, cylinder seed beads, peach moonstone, abalone fish fetishes, metal rebars and backbars; ladders, netting, single-strand fringe, overlays, reinforcing bars, braiding
Photo by Joe Van De Hatert
Model, Deshona Pepper-Robertson
Collection of Paula Hugos, Meredith Bernstein, Barbara Tober, Joanna Mandell

This necklace is one of my favorites because it just happened. It bears absolutely no resemblance to the original idea. The beads are so laden with memories of past people and places that they took on a life of their own and just sort of arranged themselves.

CAROLYN PRINCE BATCHELOR
St. Rose of Lima, 2003

12 x 17 x 1½ in. (30.5 x 43.2 x 3.8 cm)
Hand-painted paper beads, rolled individually;
sewn with metallic thread
Photo by Tom Alexander

From the series Garden Saints. *This piece
depicts St. Rose's vision of butterflies in her
rose garden. The piece opens in front, allowing
a glimpse of the saint's collaged image inside.*

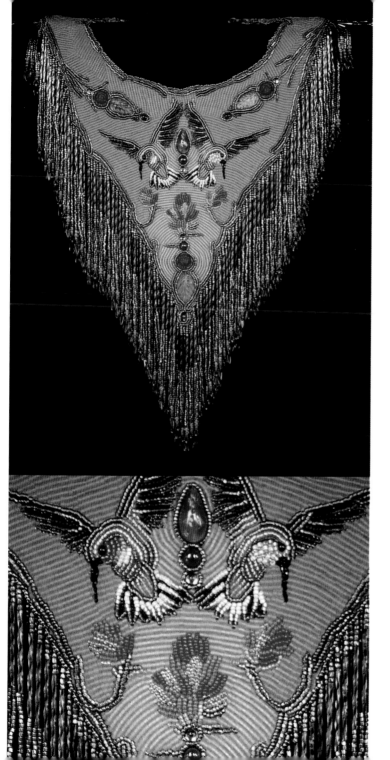

Nature inspires me daily. I hope through my work to share the beauty that surrounds me.

HEIDI F. KUMMLI
Nature's Jewels, 2001

12 x 10 x ½ in. (30.5 x 25.4 x 1.3 cm)
Seed beads, cylinder seed beads,
bugles, semiprecious stones, suedelike
fabric; bead embroidery
Photo by artist

77

SHARMINI WIRASEKARA
The Maya (Neckpiece/Wall Hanging), 2003

16 1/2 x 12 in. (41.9 x 30.5 cm)
Cylinder seed beads, bugles, hex beads, seed beads,
leather cord, wooden dowel; peyote stitch
Photo by Barbara Cohen

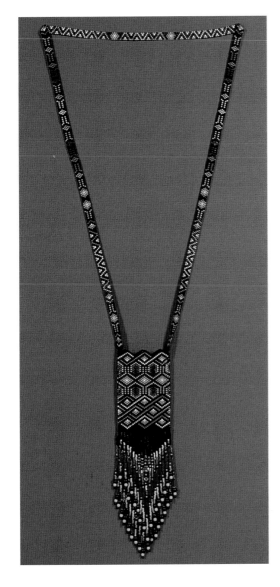

CHRIS ANN PHILIPS
Ancestral Reflections, 1998

22 x 2 in. (55.8 x 5 cm)
Cylinder seed beads, onyx, turquoise,
crystals; peyote stitch, fringe
Photo by Tom Van Eynde

PAULA WALTER
Buffalo Woman, 1997

15 x 8 x 3/4 in. (38.1 x 20.3 x 1.9 cm)
Seed beads, turquoise, amber, sterling silver, found metal,
suedelike fabric, aluminum flashing (support system),
upholstery thread; appliqué, peyote stitch, whip stitch
Photo by Kate Cameron

*The piece took more than
200 hours to complete.*

WENDY FORD
Tortoise and Hare, 2000

2½ x 6 x 4 in. (6.4 x 15.2 x 10.2 cm)
Cylinder seed beads; peyote stitch, brick stitch
Photo by Jon Van Allen

I was intrigued by the strength of peyote-stitched cylinder seed beads and wanted to create a self-supporting sculpture with the technique. The turtle's shell is hinged; an image of a hare fills the inside.

THOM ATKINS
Even Frogs Dream, 2003

5 x 18 x 11 in.
(12.7 x 45.7 x 27.9 cm)
Seed beads, novelty beads,
stuffed velvet form;
couching, backstitch
Photo by Tony Grant

I wanted to try beading a stuffed form and decided to look at the fairy tale from the frog's viewpoint.

DYAN BENDER
Earth, 2003

9½ x 9½ x 17½ in. (24.1 x 24.1 x 44.5 cm)
Seed beads, fire-polish beads, copper
sheeting, chunk native copper, antelope skull;
free-form peyote stitch
Photo by Marty Kelly

81

CHRISTINE MARTELL
Sea Turtle, 2002

22 x 9 x 10 in. (55.8 x 22.9 x 25.4 cm)
Seed beads, bugles, copper wire, wood;
free-form wirework
Photo by Diana Welch

I draw with the wire, allowing the gesture of the form to emerge. Beads add texture, emphasis, and light, bringing the sculpture to life.

WENDY ELLSWORTH
"Alang Gatang" Sea Form, 2001

4 x 4 x 4 in. (10.2 x 10.2 x 10.2 cm)
Seed beads, blown and etched
glass base; free-form herringbone
stitch, gourd stitch
Photo by David Ellsworth

*This is one in my Sea Form series,
made in components and stitched
together; there is no armature.*

DAN AND EVE KING-LEHMAN
I Am a Stone, 1980

60 x 45 in. (152.4 x 114.3 cm)
Seed beads, appliqué beads;
tapestry weave
Photo by Michael Fisher

ANN CITRON
Agile Dancer, 2002

20 x 16 x 8 in. (50.8 x 40.6 x 20.3 cm)
Seed beads, assorted beads, fabric,
wire; sewn, strung, fabric wrapped
around armature
Photo by Alex Pohl

JO ANN BAUMANN
Grandma's Garden II, 2003

12 x 7 x 2 in. (30.5 x 17.8 x 5 cm)
Seed beads, wire; Ndebele stitch
Photo by Larry Sanders

KAREN PAUST
Harvest Moon Necklace,
1999

10 x 10 x 2½ in.
(25.4 x 25.4 x 6.4 cm)
Seed beads, thread, wire;
variations on peyote stitch
Photo by T. E. Crowley
Courtesy of Mobilia Gallery

JO WOOD
My Garden, 2003

9 x 9½ x ⅜ in. (22.9 x 24.1 x .95 cm)
Seed beads, felted wool; bead embroidery
Photo by Steven M. Tiggemann,
Jeff Frey & Associates

*Seeds and weeds, bugs and bees,
and happy hands transform.
This little bit of forest becomes my
garden. I call it home.*

VIRGINIA L. BLAKELOCK
Empress, 1984

12 x 6 in. (30.5 x 15.2 cm)
Three-cut beads; loom woven
Photo by Gary L. Betts
Private collection

SUSAN ETCOFF FRAERMAN
Chance, 2003

11 x 12½ x 7½ in. (27.9 x 31.8 x 19 cm)
Seed beads, antique autograph book entry,
perforated wooden dice, nylon, linen, pigment,
thermoplastic cotton; off-loom bead weaving,
free-form right-angle weave, applied beads,
collage, thermoplastic manipulation
Photo by Tom Van Eynde
Collection of Mrs. Bonnie Gershenzon

"Diligence is the mother of good fortune," written in July 1901 in a young girl's autograph book, has been collaged into the work as testimony to the fragility of life and the swiftness of its passage.

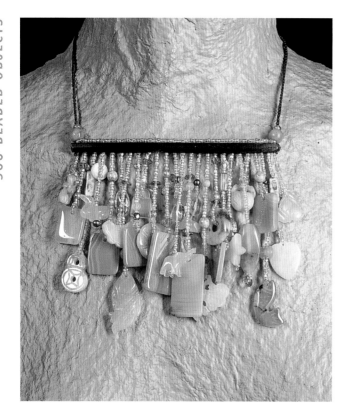

MARLA L. GASSNER
Stick Necklace, 2001

4 in. (10.2 cm)
Seed beads, "fancy" beads, jade charms
Photo by Tom Van Eynde
Collection of artist

KAREN FLOWERS
Now That's a Bead, 1995

18 in. (45.7 cm)
Seed beads, iridized lampworked
beads; strung, knotted
Photo by Tom Van Eynde

MARLA L. GASSNER
Defining Abalone, 2000

3 x 2 in. (7.6 x 5 cm)
Seed beads, "fancy" beads; helix
Photo by Tom Van Eynde
Collection of Ann Jorgensen

ELIZABETH W. RUSNELL
Interleavings, 2003

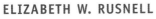

7½ x 7½ x ¼ in. (19 x 19 x .6 cm)
Ceramic and polymer clay leaves, assorted colored
glass beads, gold-wrapped thread; knotted, knitted
Photo by Aria Finch

MARCIE STONE
Neckpiece, 2003

8 x 8 x 8 in. (20.3 x 20.3 x 20.3 cm)
Assorted modern and antique seed beads,
amber, lapis lazuli and contemporary glass beads
by Karen Ovington; sculptural peyote stitch
Photo by Melva Bucksbaum

PAULA WALTER
Sacred Balance, 1998

13 x 4½ x ⅓ in. (33 x 11.4 x .8 cm)
Electroplated gold seed beads, seed beads,
malachite, copper, vermeil, brass, glass, leather,
upholstery thread; appliqué, peyote stitch,
two-bead edging
Photo by Kate Cameron
Model, Julia Acevedo
Private collection

ELEYNE WILLIAMS
Glass Dress, 2001

Twisted iridescent bugle beads,
gold-lined seed beads, assorted
seed beads, opalescent drop beads;
netting, fringe, brick stitch
Photo by Kit Williams
Collection of artist

Inspired by an Egyptian statue of a girl wearing a netted dress over a naked body, and intrigued by the possibilities of interesting shadows cast on the body, I designed this paradox of a dress—made entirely of glass! Somewhere along the way, Josephine Baker breathed the glitter and glamour of the 1920s into my design.

PAT CHIOVARIE
Fowler's Net of Amarna, 2003

19 x 11 x 1 in. (48.3 x 27.9 x 2.5 cm)
11° seed beads, semiprecious stones, silk cord;
diagonal square stitch, square stitch variations,
free netting
Photo by Joe Manfredini

*This chest piece portrays a bird
and other organic forms caught
in a marsh net from the ancient
Egyptian Amarna period.*

PAULA ANN PARMENTER
Autumn Dreams, 2002

11¼ x 6 x ¾ in. (28.5 x 15.2 x 1.9 cm)
Seed beads, hex beads, crystals, glass leaves, assorted beads, metallic thread, metal ring; square stitch, peyote stitch, fringes, Russian leaves
Photo by Larry J. Mack

These dream catchers are part of a series called Four Seasons.

PAULA ANN PARMENTER
Spring Dreams, 2001

11¼ x 6 x 1 in. (28.5 x 15.2 x 2.5 cm)
Seed beads, glass flowers and leaves,
crystals, daggers, glass butterflies,
assorted beads, metallic thread, metal
ring; square stitch, spiral stitch,
right-angle stitch, variations of peyote
stitch, fringe, netting
Photo by Larry J. Mack

DORI JAMIESON
Pink Basket, 2000

3 x 3 x 3 in. (7.6 x 7.6 x 7.6 cm)
Seed beads, drop beads; netting stitch
Photo by Lyle Jamieson

SHERRI J. THOMPSON
Beach Glass Basket #1, 2001

5½ x 6½ x 6½ in. (14 x 16.5 x 16.5 cm)
Seed beads, magatamas, tumbled beach glass;
right-angle weave
Photo by Gail Smith

*I'm a habitual beachcomber. I surrounded each piece
of beach glass with a mesh of right-angle weave, then
connected the units to form the basket.*

Nature's materials are an inspiration as well as a base for art. My beadwork uses gourds as the canvas for my designs. This piece has five beaded windows surrounding a central column of beaded bamboo, allowing it to be viewed from all sides.

SUSIE BLYSKAL
Windows, 2002

8 x 8 x 8 in. (20.3 x 20.3 x 20.3 cm)
Seed beads, gourd, bamboo;
peyote stitch, picot edging
Photo by Carl Blyskal

This piece was inspired by a trip to Tahiti, where I fell in love with their "black" pearls.

CAROL STRAUS
Tahitian Cascade, 2003

56 x ¾ x ¾ in.
(142.2 x 1.9 x 1.9 cm)
Seed beads, pearls; strung,
right-angle weave
Photo by Rick Patrick

MAGGIE ROSCHYK
Dark Mystery, 2003

18 in. (45.7 cm)
Seed beads, cylinder seed beads, Swarovski
crystals, freshwater pearls, lampworked beads
(focal bead by Kristen Frantzen Orr); netting,
peyote stitch, ladder stitch
Photo by David Orr

101

MAGGIE ROSCHYK
River to the Sea, 2003

24 in. (61 cm)
Seed beads, lampworked glass bead by Kristen Frantzen
Orr; flat Ndebele stitch, tubular Ndebele stitch, peyote
stitch, right-angle weave
Photo by David Orr

MARCIA LAGING CUMMINGS
Follow the Yellow Brick Road, 2000

9 x 8 in. (22.9 x 20.3 cm)
Seed beads, bugles, assorted beads;
peyote stitch, square stitch
Photo by Roger Bruhn

KATHERINE ROBINSON
Beaded Dreams, 2003

12 x 10 in. (30.5 x 25.4 cm)
Seed beads, bugles, drop bead, cabochon,
batik fabric, fiberfill, pillow; bead embroidery
(stacked single stitch, couching, backstitch,
lazy stitch), picot edging
Photo by Straybeads
Courtesy of Glynn-Divas Hair Gallery

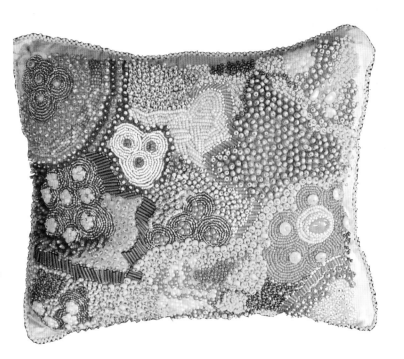

103

**DAVID K. CHATT**
Chartreuse, Orange, and Blue Bracelet, 2000

2 x 9 x 2 in (5 x 22.9 x 5 cm)
Assorted glass beads; right-angle weave
Photo by Harriet Burger

NANCY ZELLERS
*Orange, the OTHER Neutral
(An Homage to David Chatt)*, 2002

11 x 8 x 8 in. (27.9 x 20.3 x 20.3 cm)
Assorted seed beads and bugles; fringe,
right-angle weave (base)
Photo by artist

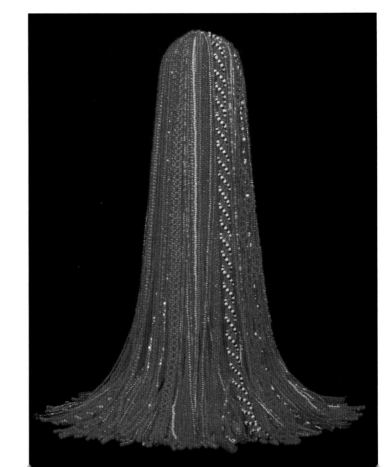

104

CHRISTINE MARIE NOGUERE
Metropolis, 2002–2003

9¾ x 6¾ x 1⅜ in. (24.7 x 17.1 x 3.5 cm)
Seed beads, wire, wool yarn, cotton yarn,
acrylic cubes, rubber rings; right-angle weave
Photo by Phil Pope

*This neck piece is inspired by Fritz Lang's
1927 film,* Metropolis, *in which a sensual
female robot incites her fellow factory
workers to riot. I imagine Maria wearing this.*

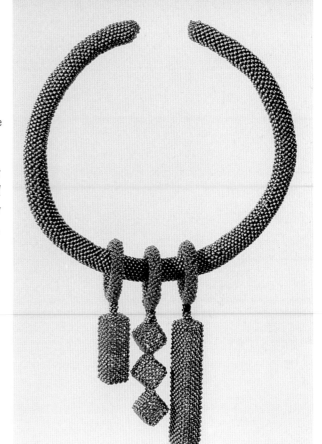

JÓH RICCI
Cubes & Spheres, 2000

26 in. (66 cm)
Cylinder seed beads, sterling silver and gold-filled beads; gourd stitch
Photo by T. R. Wailes

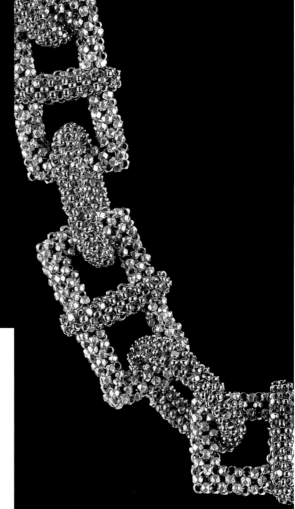

LESLIE MILTON
Chained in Duluth, 2001

20 x 1 in. (50.8 x 2.5 cm)
Vintage aluminum and gold-plated seed
beads; right-angle weave
Photo by David Egan

JACQUELINE JOHNSON
Autumn, 2002

18½ x ⅝ x ½ in. (47 x 1.6 x 1.3 cm)
Charlottes, cylinder seed beads, vermeil beads,
dichroic glass beads by Paula Radke, glass button;
tubular peyote stitch, square stitch
Photo by Joseph Giunta

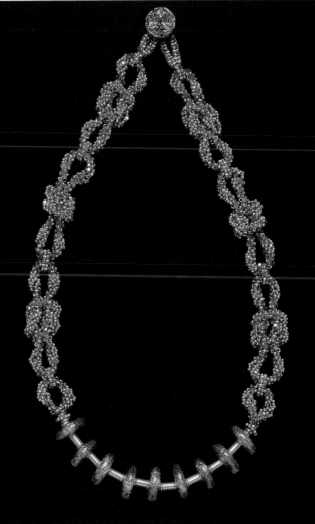

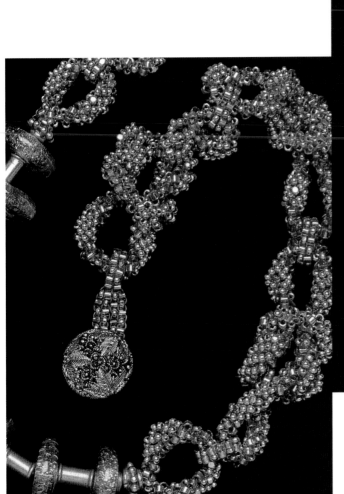

*Inspired by the memory of making
linked loop leather belts in Girl Scouts.*

107

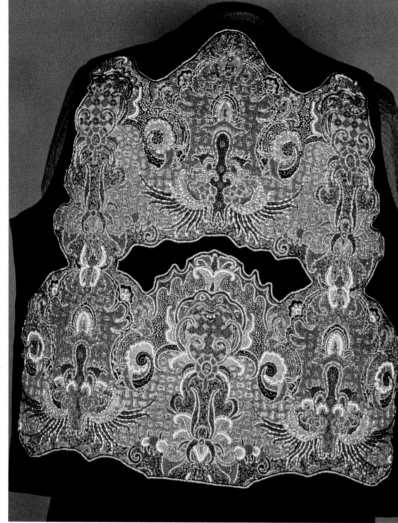

ROBERT BURNINGHAM
Beaded Vest, 1997

20 x 22 in. (50.8 x 55.8 cm)
Seed beads, assorted beads, wool crepe, metallic gold thread,
embroidery floss, silk floss; bead embroidery and embellishment,
garment construction by Charlene Burningham
Photo by Petronella Ytsma

We made this for our 50th wedding anniversary.

108

ROBERT BURNINGHAM
Beaded Jacket, 1996

21 x 21 in. (53.3 x 53.3 cm)
Seed beads, assorted beads, wool twill,
metallic gold thread, embroidery floss, silk floss;
bead embroidery, embellishment, garment
construction by Charlene Burningham
Photo by Petronella Ytsma

This project took three years to complete.

LINDA J. SOMLAI
Looking Up to See Down, 2000

23 x 15 in. (58.4 x 38.1 cm)
Seed beads, bugles, denim jacket; stitched to muslin,
mounted on jacket
Photo by Tony Somlai

RAFAEL MATIAS
Labyrinth of the Solitude, 1997

48 x 36 in. (122 x 91.4 cm)
"E" beads, ceramic tiles, wood; glued
Photo by Jill Conner

*Love and forgiveness
were my inspirations
for this piece.*

KEN TISA
It Sounds Good, 1985

72 x 42 in. (182.9 x 106.7 cm)
Glass beads, sequins, cloth, paint
Photo unattributed

111

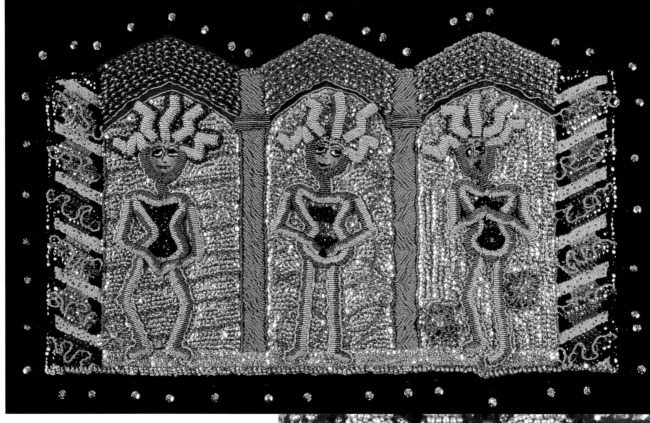

REBECCA ROUSH
*Fuck No Evil, Bear No Evil,
Nurse No Evil #2*, 1999

19 x 29 x 1 in. (48.3 x 73.6 x 2.5 cm)
Seed beads, sequins, felt; bead embroidery
Photo by Joe Manfredini

*It is a difficult title, but succinctly
states what I've come to believe
is important, and how one action
begets another. In making this
piece, I redid each figure and its
surrounding beadwork at least once;
I wanted to be completely happy
with the final work.*

MARY J. TAFOYA
Road Trip, 2001

9 x 12 in. (22.9 x 30.5 cm)
Seed beads, vintage nailheads and sequins,
laminated halftone photograph over gold linocut;
bead embroidery over suedelike fabric
Photo by Pat Berrett

Road Trip *commemorates fond
memories of an all-night drive
from Chihuahua, Mexico, to my
home in New Mexico.*

113

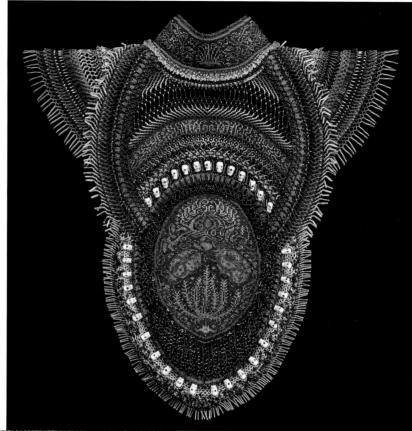

VIRGINIA L. BLAKELOCK
Calligraphy Beetles, 1987–2003

20 x 15 x ¼ in. (50.8 x 38.1 x .6 cm)
Antique seed beads, bugles;
loom woven, netting, ladders
Photo by Gary L. Betts

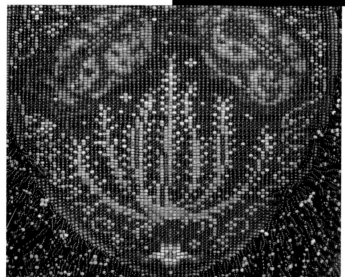

This work was originally inspired by the beetles in the oval loomed panel. Their name derives from the markings on their backs, which in turn inspired some of the calligraphic designs in the piece.

NANCY EHA
American Beauty, 1996

15 x 11 x 11 in. (38.1 x 27.9 x 27.9 cm)
Seed beads, cotton and fancy fabrics,
lace, silk flower parts, found objects;
bead embroidery
Photo by Candice Christensen

*The theme is the American
media's unrealistic expectations
of what feminine beauty is.*

EVA S. WALSH
I Am the Day, I Am the Night, 2002

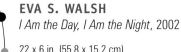

22 x 6 in. (55.8 x 15.2 cm)
Seed beads, Swarovski crystals, pearls;
loom woven, bead embroidery
Photo by Randall Smith

CONNIE LEHMAN
Tarot: I Magician, 2002

6 x 4¼ x ¼ in.
(15.2 x 10.8 x .6 cm)
Vintage French sequins,
turquoise beads, vintage
glass beads, silk noil;
bead embroidery, Russian
needle punch (*igolochkoy*)
Photo by Roger Whitacre

BETSY YOUNGQUIST
Sleeping Bear, 2003

9 x 11 x 1 in. (22.9 x 27.9 x 2.5 cm)
Seed beads, assorted beads, vintage glass
stones, acrylic ink, watercolor board; glued
Photo by Larry Sanders
Collection of Julie Tarney

SHERRY MARKOVITZ
Red Head (Rose), 2003

10 x 9 x 7 in. (25.4 x 22.9 x 17.8 cm)
Seed beads, papier-mâché, abalone; strung and glued
Photo by artist
Courtesy of Greg Kucera Gallery

SIOBHAN SHEEHAN-SULLIVAN
Mona Vanna, 2003

7½ x 6½ in. (19 x 16.5 cm)
Seed beads, garnets, amethysts, pearls,
vintage jewelry; bead embroidery, appliqué
Photo by artist

CELIA MARTIN
Following My Mewse, 2003

6 x 4½ x 4½ in. (15.2 x 11.4 x 11.4 cm)
Seed beads, fire-polish beads, shed cat whiskers,
French terry cloth, polyester stuffing; bead embroidery
Photo by artist

*Except for marking the eye placement,
the beadwork pattern was worked
entirely freehand.*

LAURA LEONARD
Woman Who Runs with Poodles, 1996

15 x 19 x 10 in. (38.1 x 48.3 x 25.4 cm)
Seed beads, fabric-wrapped wire armature,
rhinestones; peyote stitch, bead embroidery
Photo by Petronella Ytsma

*My pieces start with a stick figure made
of sculptural wire. Then fabric is wrapped
tightly around the wire to make the
shape of a figure. Beads are stitched together
to form a skin around the entire form.*

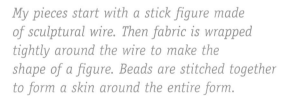

LAURA LEONARD
Martini Sister, 2002

12 x 8 x 6 in. (30.5 x 20.3 x 15.2 cm)
Seed beads, fabric-wrapped wire armature,
sculptural epoxy; peyote stitch, right-angle weave
Photo by Petronella Ytsma

LAURA LEONARD
Baba Yaga: Dedicated to the Witch in All of Us, 1999

10 x 12 x 8 in. (25.4 x 30.5 x 20.3 cm)
Seed beads, cylinder seed beads, skulls, fabric-wrapped wire armature;
peyote stitch, brick stitch, right-angle weave
Photo by Petronella Ytsma

This piece was an experiment in telling a folktale. It is very detailed, down to the frogs in the house windows. I loved the idea of a house dancing on chicken feet.

121

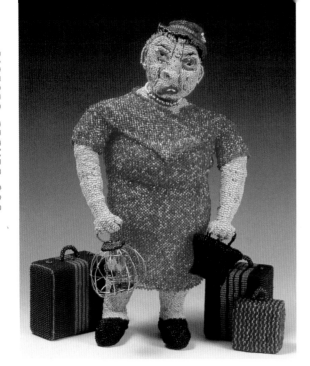

LAURA LEONARD
Mother-in-Law Cometh, 2000

14 x 10 x 8 in. (35.6 x 25.4 x 20.3 cm)
Seed beads, fabric-wrapped wire armature,
wood blocks; peyote stitch, right-angle weave
Photo by Petronella Ytsma

*This is a piece about my grandmother,
Opal, and her pet canary, Jake.
She lived with my uncle for most of
her senior years. For a laugh, I made
her much grumpier than my grandma.*

VALORIE HARLOW
Froggy Went Courting, 1999

12 x 10 x 5 in. (30.5 x 25.4 x 12.7 cm)
Seed beads, assorted beads; peyote stitch, right-angle weave
Photo by Petronella Ytsma

ANN TEVEPAUGH MITCHELL
Kosovo: Identifying the Dead, 2002

12 x 12 x 9 in. (30.5 x 30.5 x 22.9 cm)
Glass beads, glass, stones; peyote stitch,
right-angle weave, fringe, assembled
improvisationally, attached to glass vessels
Photo by Dean Powell

123

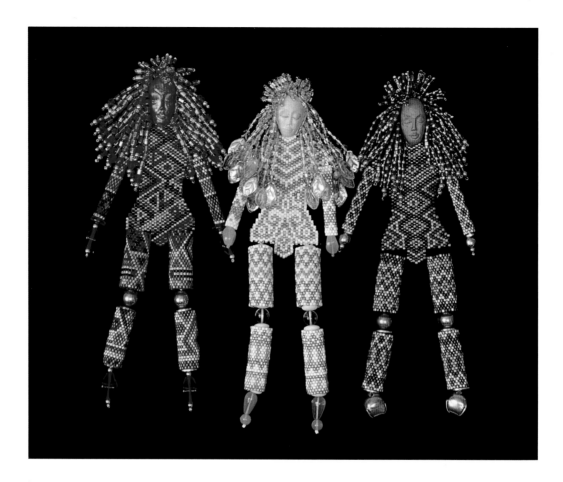

CHRISTINA MANES
Muses, 2003

2 x 6 in. (5 x 15.2 cm)
Seed beads, cylinder seed beads, assorted beads,
plastic tubing, polymer faces
Photo by Edward Matuska

*I am constantly inspired by several muses. One little muse
couldn't keep up with me, so I need several.*

I created this piece to express my feelings about the strength, power, and beauty of women I have known.

SALLY LEWIS
Goddess Triumvirate, 2003

9 x 10½ x 4½ in. (22.9 x 26.7 x 11.4 cm)
Seed beads, bugles, sequins, assorted stone
and glass cabochons, fabric, fiberfill, wood base;
couching, peyote stitch
Photo by B. Goldstein

125

SUSI JAGUDAJEV-JENKINS
Female Dragon, 2003

5 x 5 x 6 in. (12.7 x 12.7 x 15.2 cm)
Seed beads, assorted glass and stone beads,
copper wire; improvised wire weaving
Photo by Scott Parry

VALORIE HARLOW
On Dragon Wings, 2000

12 x 6 x 6 in. (30.5 x 15.2 x 15.2 cm)
Seed beads, assorted beads; peyote stitch, right-angle weave
Photo by Petronella Ytsma

This piece is made over a teapot.
The fairy creature lifts off.

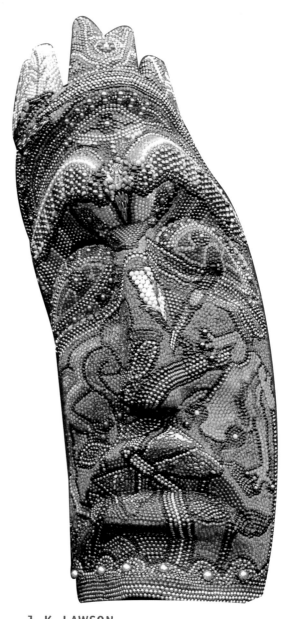

MADELYN C. RICKS
Mardi Gras Teapot, 2003

18 x 7 x 5 in. (45.7 x 17.8 x 12.7 cm)
Cylinder seed beads; peyote stitch
Photo by David Peters

*A gallery owner once told me that if a
piece has "a spout, a handle, and a lid
that comes off," it's a teapot. I love to
make beaded teapots.*

J. K. LAWSON
Jungle Spirit, 2003

66 x 24 x 24 in. (167.6 x 61 x 61 cm)
Mardi Gras beads, bamboo mask; glued
Photo by artist
Private collection

A. KIMBERLIN BLACKBURN
Ancestress, 2000

11 x 10 x 9 in. (27.9 x 25.4 x 22.9 cm)
Carved wood, acrylic paint, glass beads; laid
in paint, some beads strung with bead spinner
Photo by Robert Herold

CHARLOTTE R. MILLER
Hula Hands, 2003

6½ x 4 x ¼ in. (16.5 x 10.2 x .6 cm)
Seed beads, shells, flower beads, sterling silver head pin,
sterling silver wire; wirework, embellishment
Photo by Azad

The challenge in creating Hula Hands *was to capture the swaying motion of the grass skirt and the sensual movement of the hula in a stationary figure.*

129

AL KRUEGER
Alien Oyster, 2002

4 x 5 x 2 in. (10.2 x 12.7 x 5 cm)
Seed beads, assorted beads, pearls, modeling
compound; right-angle weave, peyote stitch
Photo by Tom Van Eynde

*I love the organic
form of this piece;
it invites viewers to
cradle it in their hands.*

ANDREA L. STERN
Encrustacean, 1998

6 x 9 x 1 in. (15.2 x 22.9 x 2.5 cm)
Seed beads, shell, turquoise beads,
pressed glass beads; bead embroidery,
fringe, peyote stitch
Photo by artist

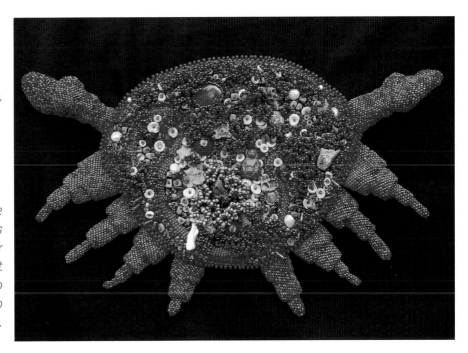

*For camouflage, some
crabs cover themselves
with objects from their
environment. This is what
a crab that wanted to
hide in my studio
would look like.*

*I used wire inside the herringbone
flower stems so that they can be
manipulated into different shapes.*

WENDY ELLSWORTH
"Tanjung Ranau" Sea Form, 2003

7 x 9 x 9 in. (17.8 x 22.9 x 22.9 cm)
Seed beads, wire, daggers; gourd stitch,
herringbone stitch
Photo by David Ellsworth

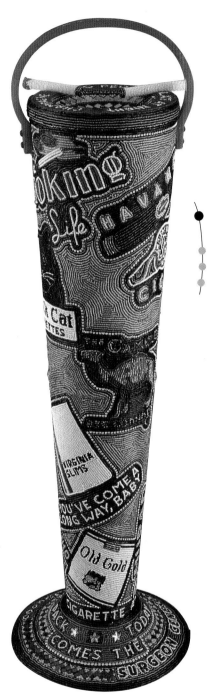

TOM WEGMAN
Beaded Ashtray, 2002

30 x 7½ in. (76.2 x 19 cm)
Seed beads, rhinestone chain, vintage ashtray; glued
Photo by David Trawick

LINDA STEVENS
Can of Pringles, 2003

9 x 3 x 3 in. (22.9 x 7.6 x 7.6 cm)
Seed beads, antique glass beads; glued
Photo by Miller Photography Inc.
Collection of Janet I. Gearin

LINDA STEVENS
Foster's Can, 2003

6¼ x 3 x 10¼ in. (15.8 x 6 x 26 cm)
Seed beads; glued
Photo by Miller Photography Inc.
Collection of Candace and Larry Trombka

The great thing about beading recycled grocery items is that you never run out of ideas for projects. The grocery store aisles are full of wonderful things to bead.

JENNIFER MOKREN
Anemone Object, 1999

9 x 6 x 6 in. (22.9 x 15.2 x 15.2 cm)
Cylinder seed beads, copper, enamel, beans; peyote stitch, electroformed and enameled copper
Photo unattributed

BETTY PAN
Black Red White, 2000

Black, 4 x 1½ in. (10.2 x 3.8 cm);
red, 3½ x 1½ in. (8.9 x 3.8 cm);
white, 3 x 1½ in. (7.6 x 3.8 cm)
Seed beads, teardrops; peyote stitch
Photo by D. James Dee

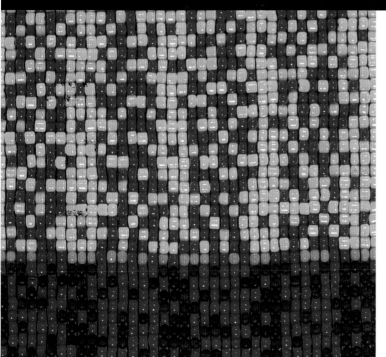

**LELAND JAY CROW
AND BARBARA L. McGONAGLE**
Coming and Going, 2001

11 x 32 x 1 in. (27.9 x 81.3 x 2.5 cm)
Seed beads; loom woven
Photo by Jeff Sabo

*We attempted to capture
the transition of an image,
the process of change, the
impermanence of objects
and ideas.*

135

JOE GIRTNER
Northwest Raven Princess, 2001

Scepter, 1 x 2 x 35 in.
(2.5 x 5 x 89 cm);
box, 4 x 6 x 22 in.
(10.2 x 15.2 x 55.8 cm)
Flaked stone, sterling silver,
wood, carved antler, vintage
seed beads; peyote stitch
Photo by artist

I did this project to show my admiration for the art and legends of the Haida and other Northwest Coast peoples.

BETH BLANKENSHIP
Fishstick, 2001

3 x ¾ x ¾ in. (7.6 x 1.9 x 1.9 cm)
Seed beads; embroidered on card stock and
glued onto recycled lipstick case
Photo by Keller's Photo Lab

I like to make artwork out of recycled containers.
I came up with the idea for Fishstick *one July, while*
focused on filling the family freezer with the salmon
that feeds us through the winter here in Alaska.

JILL GANDOLFI
Closure, 2002

6¾ x 4 x 2 in. (17.1 x 10.2 x 5 cm)
Silver precious metal clay, seed beads;
circular peyote stitch
Photo by Marty Kelly

The healed sawtooth break running across the vessel represents closure with my father, following his death in 2000.

INA GOLUB
Livyatan II, a Havdalah Spice Container, 2000

9 x 7 x 4 in. (22.9 x 17.8 x 10.2 cm)
Triangle beads, assorted beads, glass vessel,
hexolite armature; peyote stitch, herringbone stitch
Photo by Taylor Photo

CARY FRANKLIN GASPAR
African Dreams Purse, 2001

7 x 7 x 2 in. (17.8 x 17.8 x 5 cm)
Seed beads, assorted beads, antique purse frame,
antique kimono fabric, fibers; bead embroidery
Photo unattributed

ELEANORE MACNISH
"Betty Rubble" Choker, 2001

Necklace, 18 in. (45.7 cm);
largest bead, 1 x 1½ in. (2.5 x 3.8 cm)
Soda-lime hollow glass beads, sterling silver,
lampworked beads made by artist, sterling
silver chain; strung
Photo by David Nufer
Private collection

*I wanted to make something
organic but with some play value.*

MARTHA FORSYTH
Ivory & Black Mystery Bracelet, 2001

6¾ x ¼ in. (17.1 x .6 cm)
Seed beads; spiral crochet
Photo by artist

141

JACQUELINE I. LILLIE
Four-Strand Neckpiece, 1991

27½ in. (70 cm)
Antique glass beads, lathe-turned stainless steel clasps;
individually knotted
Photo by Kohl and Oláh
Private collection
Courtesy of Rosanne Raab Associates

SHARON M. DONOVAN
Stone Weave, 1996

2 x 4 in. (5 x 10.2 cm)
Sterling silver, psilomelane, silver beads, hematite beads,
onyx beads; fabricated, woven
Photo by Larry Sanders

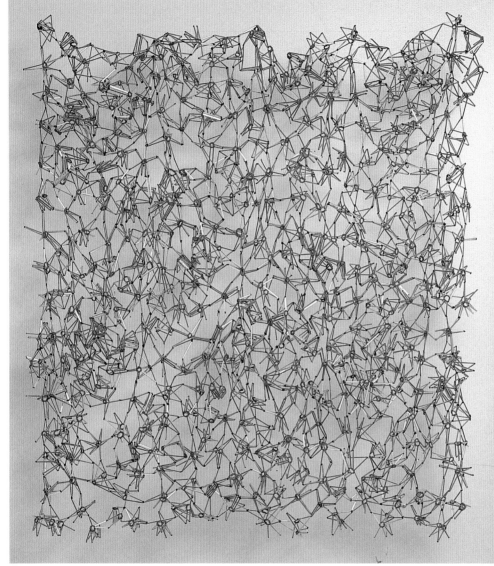

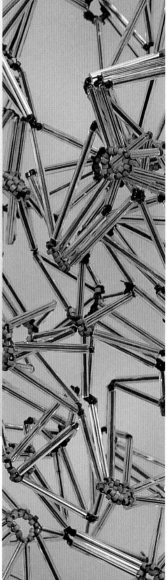

NATASHA ST. MICHAEL
Infested, 2002

31½ x 30½ x 2½ in. (80 x 77.4 x 6.4 cm)
Cylinder seed beads, bugles; peyote stitch
Photo by Paul Litherland

Inspired by the physical transformation of organic fermentation.

NATASHA ST. MICHAEL
Ferment, 2002

23½ x 19½ x 6½ in.
(59.7 x 49.5 x 16.5 cm)
Seed beads, cylinder seed
beads; circular peyote stitch
Photo by Paul Litherland

DALLAS LOVETT
Bracelet, 2002

7½ x ½ in. (19 x 1.3 cm)
Heishi and potato pearls, seed beads,
silver wire; wirework
Photo by Robert Diamante
Collection of Laurel Kubby

145

MARY HICKLIN
Lizards Swimming in Flower Puddles Bag, 1994

Bag excluding tassel: 4½ x 3¾ x ½ in.
(11.4 x 9.5 x 1.3 cm)
Seed beads, accent beads, carved onyx tassel bead;
netting, gourd stitch, daisy chain, fringe, strung
Photo by Melinda Holden
Artist's collection

NANCY KOENIGSBERG
Party Box, 2003

8 x 8 x 8 in. (20.3 x 20.3 x 20.3 cm)
Glass beads, coated copper wire;
modified soumak weave for box,
beads added with same technique
Photo by D. James Dee

147

MARCIA LAGING CUMMINGS
All Hands on Neck, 2000–2001

10 x 8 in. (25.4 x 20.3 cm)
Seed beads; peyote stitch
Photo by Roger Bruhn

MAGGIE ROSCHYK
Jewel Inside a Dream, 2003

32 in. (81.3 cm)
Seed beads, glass beads,
lampworked glass bead by
Kristen Frantzen Orr; netting
Photo by David Orr

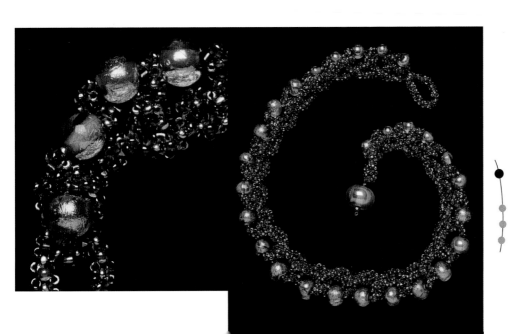

JACQUELINE JOHNSON
Crochet Necklace, 2001

15 x ⅝ x ⅜ in. (38.1 x 1.6 x .95 cm)
Charlottes, cylinder seed beads,
seed beads, dichroic glass beads by
Paula Radke; tubular peyote stitch
Photo by Joseph Giunta

This piece was inspired by the colors and shapes of the Southwest winter desert.

**LAUREL KUBBY AND
DALLAS LOVETT**
Organic Desert, 2002

Necklace, 20 in. (50.8 cm);
pendant, 5 x 2½ in. (12.7 x 6.4 cm)
Seed beads, potato and heishi pearls, gold wire;
herringbone stitch, peyote stitch, wirework
Photo by Robert Diamante

SALLY SHORE
Summertime, 2003

42½ in. (107.9 cm)
Seed beads, drop beads, daggers;
triple helix, fringe
Photo by artist

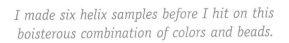

I made six helix samples before I hit on this boisterous combination of colors and beads.

DONA ANDERSON
Caught in a Net Bracelet, 2002

Box, 1 x 3 in. (2.5 x 7.6 cm); rope, 18 in. (45.7 cm)
Cylinder seed beads, assorted seed beads, pearls, crystals, bugles, accent beads, topaz;
tubular herringbone stitch, three-dimensional right-angle weave
Photo by Ron Bez

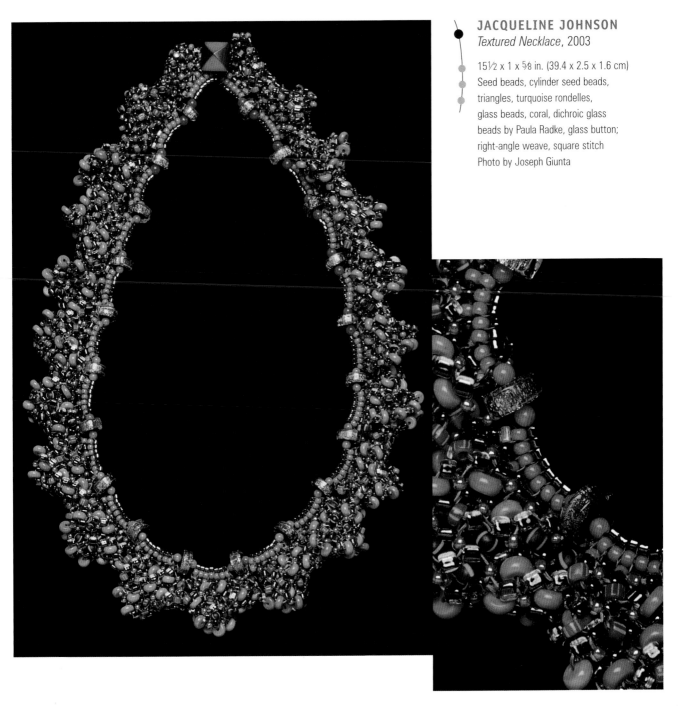

JACQUELINE JOHNSON
Textured Necklace, 2003

15½ x 1 x ⅝ in. (39.4 x 2.5 x 1.6 cm)
Seed beads, cylinder seed beads,
triangles, turquoise rondelles,
glass beads, coral, dichroic glass
beads by Paula Radke, glass button;
right-angle weave, square stitch
Photo by Joseph Giunta

ANN TEVEPAUGH MITCHELL
Wading In, 2003

16 x 10 x 7 in. (40.6 x 25.4 x 17.8 cm)
Glass beads, kelp stem, stones; peyote stitch assembled
dimensionally and improvisationally, right-angle weave and
netting also sewn improvisationally
Photo by Dean Powell

DONNA L. LISH
Undertow, 2003

5 x 45 x 26 in. (12.7 x 114.3 x 66 cm)
Square beads; netting
Photo by artist

Auntie gives thanks standing in the water, the elixir that feeds her grove, while her companion learns a few of her tried and true teachings.

A. KIMBERLIN BLACKBURN
Auntie and Big Boy in the Grove, 2001

21 x 15 x 18 in. (53.3 x 38.1 x 45.7 cm)
Carved wood, acrylic paint, glass beads; laid in paint,
some beads strung with bead spinner
Photo by artist

156

DAVID J. ROIDER
Mola Fish, 2003

4 x 5½ in. (10.2 x 25.4 cm)
Cylinder seed beads; peyote stitch
Photo by artist

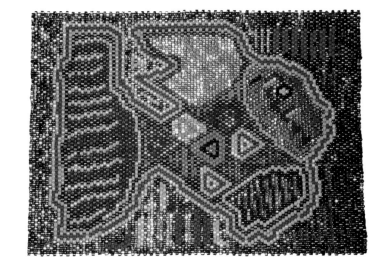

SARABETH CULLINAN
Sunset Colors Captured, 2003

1½ x 3¼ x 2 in. (3.8 x 8.2 x 5 cm)
Seed beads, semiprecious beads (amethyst,
carnelian, topaz, citrine), rock; peyote stitch,
peyote ruffle, embellishment
Photo by Robert Still

*Capturing one fleeting moment of a capricious sunset was
my reason for beading an ordinary rock with the rich,
fiery colors of purple, violet, orange, and yellow.*

157

JILL ACKIRON-MOSES
Encrustacean Cuff Bracelet, 2003

3½ x 7½ in. (8.9 x 19 cm)
Seed beads, bugles, suedelike fabric,
sterling silver and pearl clasp;
bead embroidery
Photo by Hap Sakwa

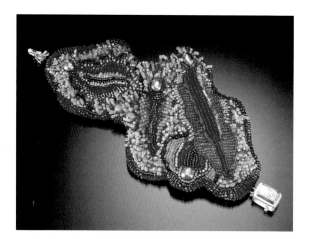

JILL ACKIRON-MOSES
Seduction Cuff Bracelet, 2003

3½ x 7 in. (8.9 x 17.8 cm)
Seed beads, sequins, freshwater
pearls, suedelike fabric, sterling
silver and pearl clasp;
bead embroidery
Photo by Hap Sakwa

**MARGIE DEEB AND
FRIEDA BATES**
Dance of the Undines, 2003

29 x 21 x 7 in. (73.6 x 53.3 x 17.8 cm)
Seed beads, acrylic stand, glass rocks;
loom woven
Designed by Margie Deeb; executed
by Margie Deeb and Frieda Bates
Photo by John Haigwood

*This piece is a
study of movement
through pattern.*

159

RUTH M. McCORRISON
Cottonwood Creek, Winter, 2002

11 x 5½ in. (27.9 x 14 cm)
Cylinder seed beads; loom woven
Photo by Steve Odendahl
Collection of Wichita Center for the Arts

*I took the photograph from which this piece is derived while standing
on the ice on the creek near my house one winter at dusk.*

JO WOOD
Snow Stripes, 2002

10¾ x 9 x ⅜ in. (27.3 x 22.9 x .95 cm)
Seed beads, felted wool; bead embroidery
Photo by Steven M. Tiggemann, Jeff Frey & Associates

Trudging up a well-packed trail, my attention is drawn to the blink and flash, a pattern of bright light and shadow. I find myself gliding through snow stripes, going home.

161

I tried to incorporate all the stitches I know into this piece.

REBECCA BROWN-THOMPSON
Leaf Lei, 2003

14 x 7½ in. (35.5 x 19 cm)
Seed beads, assorted beads, cord; right-angle weave,
peyote stitch, brick stitch, herringbone stitch, square stitch
Photo by Murray Irwin

LESLIE CIECHANOWSKI
World Fair, 1998

11 x 6 x 4 in. (27.9 x 15.2 x 10.2 cm)
Seed beads, vase, polystyrene foam balls, wire;
right-angle weave
Photo by Larry Stessin

LESLIE CIECHANOWSKI
Zamboodo Dancer, 1998

15 x 5 x 5 in. (38.1 x 12.7 x 12.7 cm)
Seed beads, assorted glass beads, bottle, wire; right-angle weave
Photo by Larry Stessin

163

LIZ MANFREDINI
Pea Pod Brooch and Stand, 1995

6½ x 5⅝ x 1 in. (16.5 x 14.2 x 2.5 cm)
Seed beads; peyote stitch, square stitch, bead embroidery
Photo by Joe Manfredini

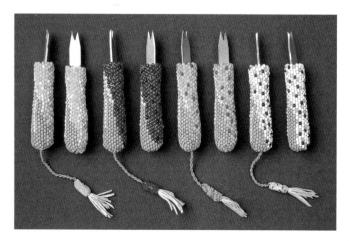

CAROL PERRENOUD
Corn for Dinner, 1995

9 x 11 x 2½ in. (22.9 x 27.9 x 6.4 cm);
each holder, 4 in. (10.2 cm)
Seed beads, corn cob holders, suedelike fabric;
peyote stitch, bead embroidery
Photo by artist

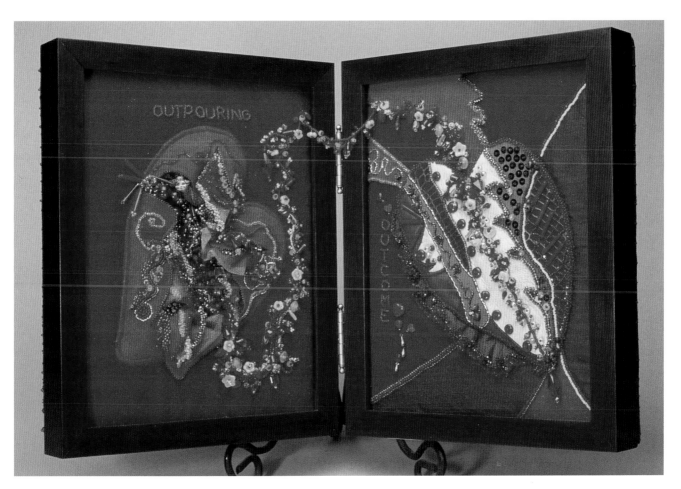

SANDRA JAECH
It's Never the Same, 2002

10½ x 16½ x 2 in. (26.7 x 41.9 x 5 cm)
Seed beads, assorted glass and semiprecious beads;
bead embroidery, fringe, quilting
Photo by Joe Manfredini

The two-sided format is used to convey the contrast between an artist's "outpouring" of effort and emotion to create a piece and the piece's eventual "outcome."

165

DIANE FITZGERALD
Rose Garden Hat, 2002

5 x 15 x 15 in. (12.7 x 38.1 x 38.1 cm)
Seed beads, cylinder seed beads
Photo by artist

MARCIA KATZ
Snake Hatband, 1999

28 x 4 x 1½ in. (71.1 x 10.2 x 3.8 cm)
Seed beads, triangle beads,
assorted beads; flat, tubular,
circular, and sculptural peyote
stitch, fringe, netting
Photo by Peter Gorman

167

CINDY WROBEL
Chrysalis—Birth of Creativity, 2001

26 x 8 x 7 in. (66 x 20.3 x 17.8 cm)
Assorted beads, wire, wood; strung on wire
and wrapped around wire framework and
carved wood form
Photo by Jim Sokolik

*Inside a cocoon awaits something
of incredible beauty. Out of
something plain and simple,
wonder and greatness can appear.
We all have this possibility
inside us.*

JUDY SAYE-WILLIS
Color Play, 2002

16 x 2 x ¾ in. (40.6 x 5 x 1.9 cm)
Seed beads, fused glass by
Kellylynn Robitaille; crochet
Photo by Tom Stanley

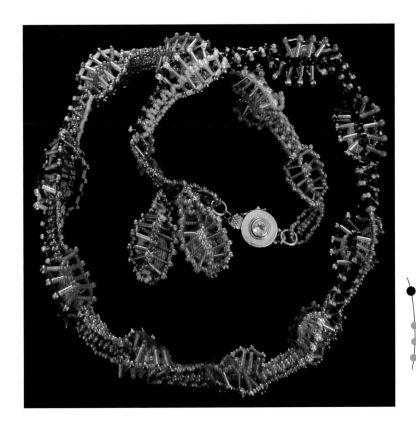

GILLIAN LAMB
Chevrons, 2002

Necklace, 28 in. (71.1 cm);
earrings, 1½ x 2¾ in. (3.8 x 6.9 cm)
Seed beads, bugles, crystals,
hex beads, accent beads;
three-sided chevron chain stitch
Photo by artist

JACQUELINE JOHNSON
Eyelet Necklace, 2001

21 x 1½ x ¼ in. (53.3 x 3.8 x .6 cm)
Charlottes, cylinder seed beads,
dichroic beads by Paula Radke;
right-angle weave, square stitch
Photo by Steve Meltzer

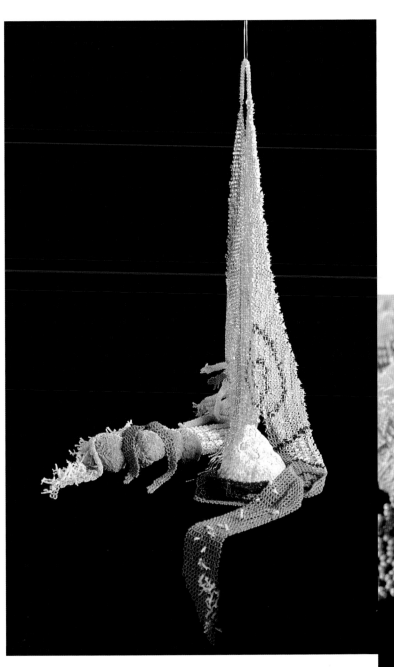

ELEANOR LUX
Plein Aire Justice, 2001

18 x 8 x 10 in. (45.7 x 20.3 x 25.4 cm)
Seed beads, sequins, coral, found objects;
right-angle weave and peyote stitch
Photo by Cindy Momchilou

LAUREN HARVEY
Iona Sea Bag, 2002

5 x 2⅜ in. (12.7 x 6 cm)
Cylinder seed beads, bugles,
seed beads, embellishment beads,
mother-of-pearl; two-drop
peyote stitch, branched fringe
Photo by Tom Van Eynde

ANGELA RIEHL
Bargello Bag, 2000

Pouch, 5¼ in. (13.3 cm); overall, 41 in. (104.1 cm)
Cylinder seed beads, shell, copper, crystals, seed beads;
three-drop peyote stitch
Photo by Angi Riehl

GINI WILLIAMS
Solomon's Wedding, 1999

25 x 6 x ¼ in. (63.5 x 15.2 x .6 cm)
Charlottes, antique bugles, pearl, cathedral glass
beads, pressed glass beads; loom woven,
bead embroidery, peyote stitch, fringe
Photo by Alan Miller

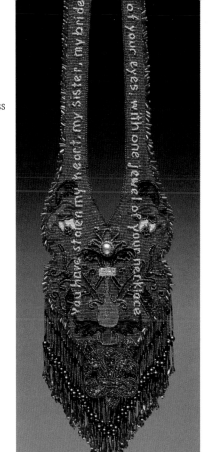

PAULA ANN PARMENTER
Celtic Forest, 2000

17 x 4 x ¾ in. (43.2 x 10.2 x 1.9 cm)
Seed beads, crystals, glass flowers and leaves; spiral stitch,
chevron stitch, peyote stitch, variation of herringbone stitch,
netting, fringe
Photo by Larry J. Mack

173

LUCIA ANTONELLI
Rio Abajo Rio—a River Beneath the River, 1993

Necklace, 19 in. (48.3 cm);
centerpiece, 2½ x 2¾ in. (6.4 x 6.9 cm)
Antique French brass beads, new and antique glass beads, handmade silver pendants, antique silver and bronze beads, carnelian, imperial jasper, leather, sterling silver centerpiece by artist; silverwork, strung, hand-stitching (lazy stitch)
Photo by artist

I love primitive tribal jewelry. Its funky nature inspired me to fabricate my own centerpiece, bringing the necklace into the present with a contemporary edge while maintaining a primitive quality.

VIRGINIA L. BLAKELOCK
Crude Root, 1988

16 x 9 x 1 in. (40.6 x 22.9 x 2.5 cm)
Three-cut beads; loom woven, peyote stitch, ladders, kinky fringe
Photo by Alice Korach

175

JOANNE STREHLE BAST
Princesses on Pointe, 2000

12½ x 8½ x 8½ in. (31.8 x 21.6 x 21.6 cm)
Seed beads, assorted beads, magatamas,
squares, triangles, pointe shoe; right-angle weave,
peyote stitch, bead embroidery, square stitch
Photo by T. R. Wailes

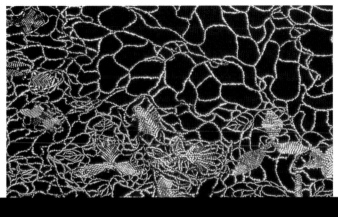

PAT CHIOVARIE
Forest Maiden's Wedding Veil and Tiara, 2002

Veil, 24 x 25 x 1 in. (61 x 63.5 x 2.5 cm);
tiara, 21 x 4 x 1 in. (53.3 x 10.2 x 2.5 cm)
Seed beads, semiprecious stones; diagonal square stitch,
free netting, brick stitch, herringbone stitch
Photo by Joe Manfredini

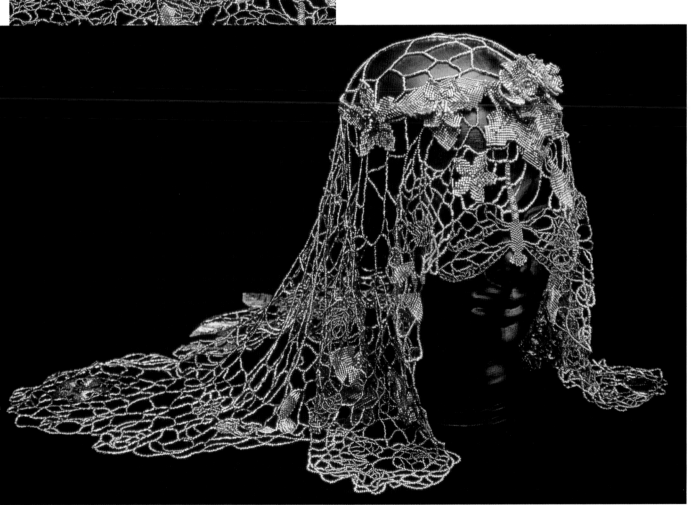

SHERRY SERAFINI
Spike, 2003

6 x 14 in. (15.2 x 35.6 cm)
Agate cabochons, cylinder seed beads,
seed beads, suedelike fabric; bead embroidery,
surface embellishment with spike fringe
Photo by Kevin P. Ritchey

SHANTASA SALING
Persephone, 2002

16 x 8 x 2 in. (40.6 x 20.3 x 5 cm)
Cylinder seed beads, seed beads, manzanita branch;
peyote stitch, Dutch spiral, Russian leaves
Photo by artist

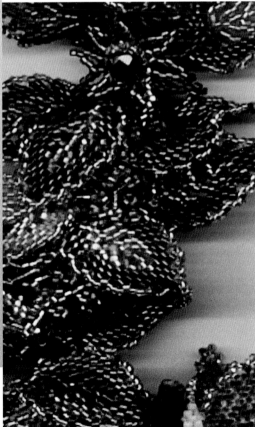

179

HEIDI F. KUMMLI
Solstice, 2001

14 x 4½ x ½ in. (35.6 x 11.4 x 1.3 cm)
Seed beads, cylinder seed beads, bugles,
turquoise, bone stick, art glass by Bruce
St. John Maher, suedelike fabric;
bead embroidery
Photo by artist

DONNA ZAIDENBERG
Autumn Leaves, 1998

20 x 3 in. (50.8 x 7.6 cm)
Glass beads, pearls, crystals,
copper beads and closure;
free-form peyote stitch
Photo by Tom Van Eynde

MICHELLE RILEY
Heart-Shaped Beaded Purse, 2002–2003

6½ x 5 in. (16.5 x 12.7 cm)
Seed beads, assorted glass
beads, fabric; bead embroidery, fringe
Photo by Tom Ricketts

SUSAN HILLYER
That Purse with a Ruffle, 2002

7 x 5 x 5 in. (17.8 x 12.7 x 12.7 cm)
Cylinder seed beads, silver cuts; herringbone stitch
Photo by artist

*This was inspired by a memory of a rag
drawstring purse that I played with as a child.
Making it took me on a journey of healing
my relationship with my mother.*

KATHLEEN BOLAN
Birth Day, 2000

2¼ x 2¼ x 2¼ in. (5.7 x 5.7 x 5.7 cm)
Seed beads, charlottes, heart bead,
polymer face, ribbon; square stitch,
brick stitch, edge stitch
Photo by Tim Thayer

The EKG heartbeat peaks at birth.
New life has a face that looks both new and old.
It springs forth, bringing joy and celebration.

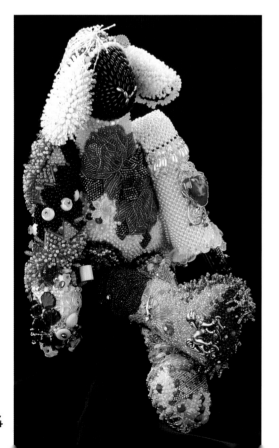

DEBRA SMITH
Lamby, 1998

15 x 7 x 3½ in. (38.1 x 17.8 x 8.9 cm)
Assorted glass, gemstone, and lampworked beads,
stuffed linen animal; peyote stitch, brick stitch,
right-angle weave, couching, bead embroidery
Photo by Chris Arend

I wanted to bead something that I could put all my
emotions into and that would embrace the things in
my life that are important to me.

NORRIS DALTON
*Porcelain Beaded Necklace with
Face Medallion*, 1982

Necklace, 16 x ¾ x ⁵⁄₁₆ in. (40.6 x 1.9 x .8 cm);
medallion, 2 x 2 x ¾ in. (5 x 5 x 1.9 cm)
Hand-formed porcelain beads,
appliqué face medallion; strung
Photo by Michael Crow

NORRIS DALTON
*Porcelain Beaded Necklace with
Face Medallion*, 1982

Necklace, 16 x ¾ x ⁵⁄₁₆ in. (40.6 x 1.9 x .8 cm);
medallion, 2 x 2 x ¾ in. (5 x 5 x 1.9 cm)
Hand-formed porcelain beads,
appliqué face medallion; strung
Photo by Michael Crow

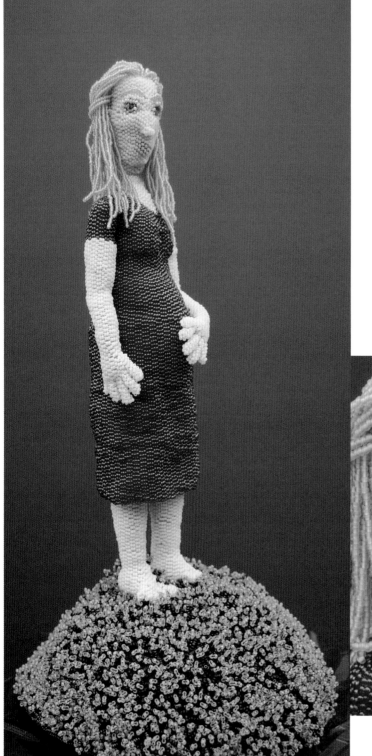

COLLEEN O'ROURKE
Eve of Uncertainty, 2002

15 x 8 x 8 in. (38.1 x 20.3 x 20.3 cm)
Seed beads; peyote stitch
Photo by Thomas O'Rourke

*I moved across the country
the day after I found out
I was pregnant with my first child.
Traveling with me were the
uncertainty and doubts that new
mothers face. "Will I be a good mother?"
"Is the baby healthy?" This piece
helped me work through those
issues—so did my beautiful child.*

LIZ MANFREDINI
There Was an Old Lady, 1996

10 x 4 x 3 in. (25.4 x 10.2 x 7.6 cm)
Seed beads; peyote stitch,
right-angle weave, bead embroidery
Photo by Joe Manfredini

NOME F. M. MAY
She Chose Both, 2002

12½ x 6½ x ¼ in. (31.8 x 16.5 x .6 cm)
Antique seed beads, antique aluminum
beads, sugilite, pearls, sterling silver;
bead embroidery, strung
Photo by Martin Kilmer
Collection of Paula Walters

*I made this piece in honor of my
friend Karen Buston, who passed
away from breast cancer. The
dignity and humor with which
she faced her mortality continue
to inspire me. Together we chose
this image as the true representation
of her spirit.*

KAREN BRUNER
Winged Protectress, 2001

5½ x 8½ x 5 in. (14 x 21.6 x 12.7 cm)
Cylinder seed beads, seed beads, pressed
glass beads, clay armature; peyote stitch,
Xhosa double-sided scallop stitch
Photo by Marcia Major-Albert, Catch Light Studios

MARY J. TAFOYA
Shepherdess Angel, 2000

6 x 7 x ⅜ in. (15.2 x 17.8 x .95 cm); strap, 16 in. (40.6 cm)
Seed beads, vintage steel cut beads, metal and other sequins, gemstone and trade beads, assorted embellishments and findings, brass wire, brass bells, raw silk; bead embroidery over trapunto quilting
Photo by Pat Berrett

Trapunto quilting is an easy way to create a multidimensional surface for a bead embroidery project.

NanC MEINHARDT
Between a Rock and a Hard Place, 2001

12 x 8 x 5 in. (30.5 x 20.3 x 12.7 cm)
Seed beads, gold beads, modeling compound, polymer clay,
terra-cotta; free-form right-angle weave
Photo by Tom Van Eynde

My beadwork represents psychological fables.

ANN TEVEPAUGH MITCHELL
Bathing Beauty #1, 1998

7 x 10 x 17 in. (17.8 x 25.4 x 43.2 cm)
Glass beads, kelp stem, shell, glass; peyote stitch,
brick stitch, assembled improvisationally
Photo by Dean Powell

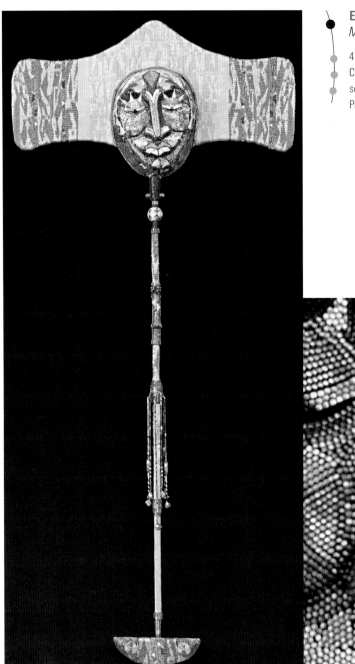

ELFLEDA RUSSELL
Memory Mask, 2001

47 x 21 x 4 in. (119.3 x 53.3 x 10.2 cm)
Cylinder seed beads, plaster, papier-mâché, wood form;
sculptural peyote stitch, card weaving
Photo by artist

COLLIS CAROLINE MARSHALL
Salvador Dolly Lama, 2002

10½ x 8 x 5 in. (26.7 x 20.3 x 12.7 cm)
Vintage bone buttons, bone heart beads,
seed beads, bugles, vintage crystal and glass
beads, fabric, vegetable ivory; bead embroidery,
brick stitch, ladder stitch
Photo by Geoff Carr

VIRGINIA BRUBAKER
The Goddess Who Weaves the Night Sky, 2003

13 x 15 in. (33 x 38.1 cm)
Seed beads, assorted glass and stone beads, acrylic paint; brick stitch
Photo by artist

BETSY YOUNGQUIST
Surfacing, 2003

15 x 14 x 1 in. (38.1 x 35.6 x 2.5 cm)
Seed beads, assorted beads, vintage glass stones, acrylic ink, watercolor board; glued
Photo by Larry Sanders

MIMI HOLMES
Decorative Pattern:
Lost in a See of Words, 2001

14¾ x 12 x ¾ in. (37.5 x 30.5 x 1.9 cm)
Sequins, assorted beads,
bead and fabric trim;
photo transfer, bead embroidery
Photo by artist

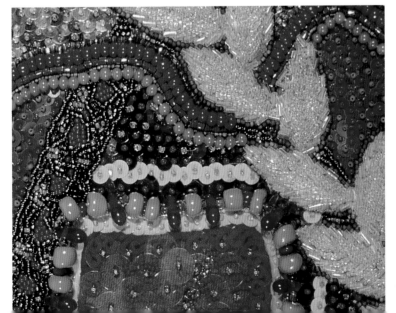

195

AMY C. CLARKE
Apple, 2001

5½ x 5½ in. (14 x 14 cm)
Seed beads, fabric; bead embroidery (backstitch)
Photo by Joe Coca
Collection of Sara and David Lieberman

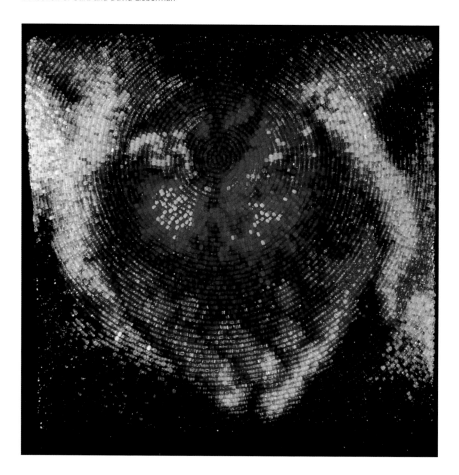

*So many stories contain apples. I've always been fascinated
with how, in myths and fairy tales, everyday objects such as
apples take on magical qualities.*

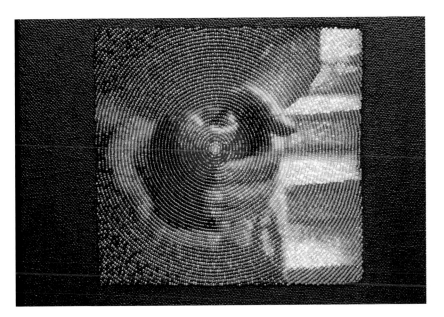

AMY C. CLARKE
Apple with Stairs, 2001

4½ x 5 in. (11.4 x 12.7 cm)
Seed beads, fabric;
bead embroidery (backstitch)
Photo by artist
Collection of Cathy and Marty Wise

I love the purple-reds and orange-reds in the skin of an apple. I love the full shape; it is heartlike. I love the simple brown stem; it is the umbilical connection to a tree.

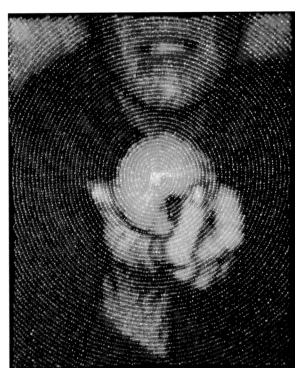

AMY C. CLARKE
Bite?, 2003

4¾ x 5½ in. (12 x 14 cm)
Seed beads, fabric;
bead embroidery (backstitch)
Photo by artist
Collection of Darcy Walker

LAURA WILLITS
Plunge, 2001

19 x 12 in. (48.3 x 30.5 cm)
Seed beads; loom woven
Photo by Philip Arny

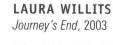
LAURA WILLITS
Journey's End, 2003

20⅛ x 9¼ in. (50.8 x 23.5 cm)
Seed beads; loom woven
Photo by Philip Arny

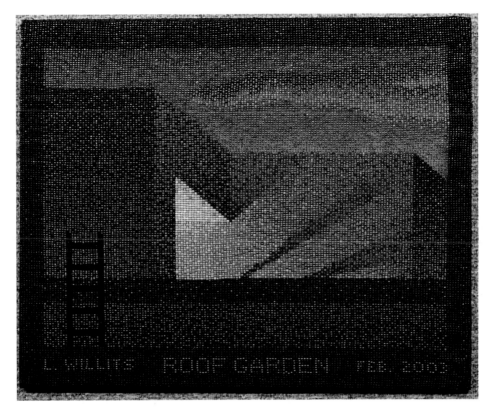

LAURA WILLITS
Roof Garden, 2003

11 x 13⅞ in. (27.9 x 35.2 cm)
Seed beads; loom woven
Photo by Philip Arny

I could just see the elevator "house" at the top of the building and wondered how it might look at night.

199

MARGO C. FIELD
Flowers for Helene, 2000

4½ x 20 x 10 in. (11.4 x 50.8 x 25.4 cm)
Seed beads, cactus wood, wire armatures;
herringbone stitch, peyote stitch,
invented weaving techniques
Photo by Pat Berrett

NANCY GOLDBERG
Hibiscus in Cloisonné,
2002

23 x 20 x 12 in.
(58.4 x 50.8 x 30.5 cm)
Seed beads, garnets;
French and Victorian
beaded flower techniques
Photo by James Lasley

*The natural beauty
of flowers inspires
me to re-create and
preserve that beauty
through art.*

KAREN PAUST
Susan's Hibiscus Brooch, 2002

4½ x 5 x 4 in. (11.4 x 12.7 x 10.2 cm)
Seed beads, lentil glass beads, thread, wire, sterling silver pin back;
variations on peyote stitch, netting
Photo by T. E. Crowley

I love irises because they're so beautiful and are called "the poor man's orchid."

KAREN PAUST
Iris II Brooch, 2001

7 x 4 x 3 in. (17.8 x 10.2 x 7.6 cm)
Seed beads, wire, sterling silver pin back;
variations on peyote stitch, Ndebele stitch
Photo by T. E. Crowley

DONNA DEANGELIS DICKT
Sunflowers, 2003

20 x 30 x 12 in. (50.8 x 76.2 x 30.5 cm)
Seed beads, three-cuts;
French flower beading
Photo by artist

JO WOOD
Dragonflies and Dandelions, 2003

11½ x 8¼ x ⅜ in. (29.2 x 21 x .95 cm)
Seed beads, felted wool; bead embroidery
Photo by Steven M. Tiggemann, Jeff Frey & Associates

*Ah, spring! Settled on my cabin step, I breathe in springtime
and witness the dance of this season, of dragonflies and dandelions.*

SAGE ZERING
Conch Shell, 2001

5 x 12 x 7 in. (12.7 x 30.5 x 17.8 cm)
Seed beads; peyote stitch
Photo by Steve Talmadge

A.KIMBERLIN BLACKBURN
Homeland Meandering, 2001

12 x 7½ x 9 in. (30.5 x 19 x 22.9 cm)
Carved wood, acrylic paint, glass beads;
laid in paint, some beads strung with bead spinner
Photo by artist

Palms sway on either side of the stream that keeps the flowers in bloom.

A.KIMBERLIN BLACKBURN
In the Taro Patch, 1999

21 x 13 x 10 in. (53.3 x 33 x 25.4 cm)
Carved wood, acrylic paint, glass beads;
laid in paint, some beads strung with bead spinner
Photo by Robert Herold
Collection of Hawaii State Foundation on Culture and the Arts

WENDY ELLSWORTH
"Selat Bangka" Sea Form, 2002

6 x 5 x 4 in. (15.2 x 12.7 x 10.2 cm)
Seed beads, antique pressed glass beads,
assorted beads; free-form herringbone stitch,
gourd stitch
Photo by David Ellsworth
Collection of Joan Borenstein

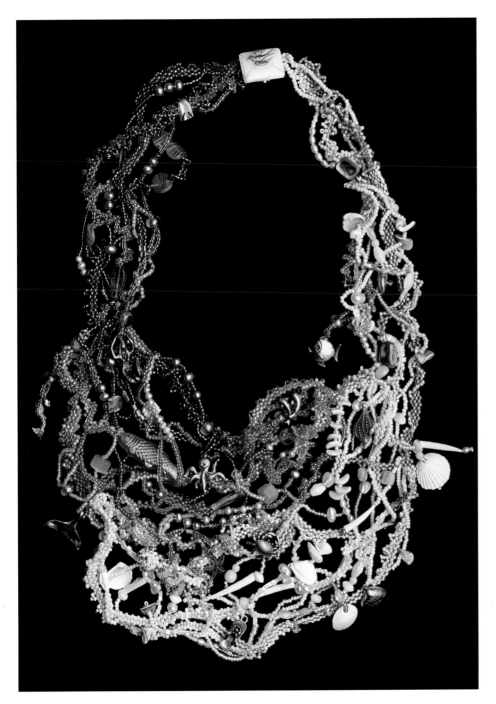

The ocean, beach, and water continue to influence my beaded designs. I wanted to put all the elements into one necklace.

JOANNE McFARLAND
Ocean Front, 2002

25 x 6 in.
(63.5 x 15.2 cm)
Seed beads, shells,
charms, assorted beads;
free-form peyote stitch
Photo by Rick Nelson

209

KATE ROTHRA
Terrestrial Anemone Necklace, 2003

17½ in. (44.5 cm)
Handblown lampworked glass beads
Photo by Ralph Gabriner

I scrapped this piece so many times before I arrived at the desired effect. I wanted the colors to play off of each other, to create a sort of buzz from color placement alone.

RONNIE LAMBROU
Gemstone Twist, 2003

18 in. (45.7 cm)
Seed beads, assorted glass and stone beads,
hollow lampworked beads by Jeri Warhaftig,
wire, vermeil cones and clasp;
strung, wirework
Photo by Panos Lambrou

SUZANNE GOLDEN
Evolution #2, 2003

5½ x 5½ x 1¾ in.(14 x 14 x 4.4 cm)
Seed beads; tubular peyote stitch
Photo by artist

SUZANNE GOLDEN
Evolution #3, 2003

5 x 5 x 1¼ in. (12.7 x 12.7 x 3.2 cm)
Seed beads; tubular peyote stitch
Photo by artist

SUZANNE GOLDEN
Evolution #4, 2003

5 x 5 x 1¾ in. (12.7 x 12.7 x 4.4 cm)
Seed beads; tubular peyote stitch
Photo by artist

SUZANNE GOLDEN
Evolution #5, 2003

4¼ x 4¼ x 1⅛ in. (10.8 x 10.8 x 2.6 cm)
Seed beads; tubular peyote stitch
Photo by artist

In the Evolution *series, I wanted to use the tubular peyote technique and varying bead sizes to create bold designs using only black and white beads.*

BILLIE JEAN THEIDE
Victory, 2000

32 in. (81.2 cm)
Cylinder seed beads; peyote stitch
Photo by artist

DORI JAMIESON
Emergence, 1999

4 x 3 x 3 in. (10.2 x 7.6 x 7.6 cm)
Seed beads, garnet chips; peyote stitch
Photo by Lyle Jamieson

*The bead colors and contrast
drove the making of this piece.*

215

MARTHA FORSYTH
Reversible Ivory & Black Necklace with Daggers, 1999

16½ in. (41.9 cm)
Seed beads, drop beads, daggers, accent bead, gold-filled wire; spiral crochet, clasp wirework
Photo by artist

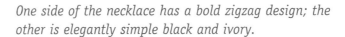

One side of the necklace has a bold zigzag design; the other is elegantly simple black and ivory.

SHARRI MOROSHOK
Turquoise Inspiration, 2002

24 in. (60.9 cm)
Seed beads, charlottes,
cylinder seed beads;
peyote stitch
Photo by Brian McLernon

217

NIKIA ANGEL
Untitled, 2001

1½ x 1½ in. (3.8 x 3.8 cm)
Wooden beads, seed beads, assorted accent beads,
silver Bali beads, vintage Swarovski crystals, lampworked beads
by Bernadette Fuentes; peyote stitch and variations
Photo by Pat Berrett

KAY DOLEZAL
Collar and Low Box, 2002

Collar, 15 x 15 in. (38.1 x 38.1 cm);
box, 6 x 6 in. (15.2 x 15.2 cm)
Seed beads; right-angle weave
Photo by Steve Gyurina

*I made the low box to
hold the collar. When the
collar is spread out flat,
the box can be turned
upside down and placed
in the center to create
a new design for display.*

MARTHA C. NIKLA

Beaded Reflections, 2003

22 x 9 x 1¾ in. (55.8 x 22.9 x 4.4 cm)
Swarovski crystals, Swarovski disc beads, mirrored discs,
enameled metal beads, sterling silver tambourine beads,
wire, mirror; wirework
Photo by Tom McCarthy

*I made this as a charitable contribution for a
breast cancer research fundraiser. Contributing
artists were asked to embellish a mirror.*

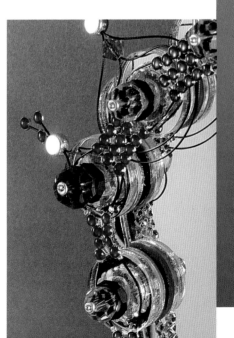

219

CAROL DE BOTH
*White Centipedes Joined
at the Hips*, 2000

2½ x 7½ in. (6.4 x 19 cm)
Seed beads, safety pins, sterling
silver neck ring; right-angle weave,
peyote spikes
Photo by Tom Van Eynde
Courtesy of Morgan Contemporary
Glass Gallery

*Hard glass beads are sewn together and
magically become a fuzzy necklace!*

NANCY KOENIGSBERG
Untitled, 1985

3¼ x 4½ x 4½ in. (8.2 x 11.4 x 11.4 cm)
Glass beads, plastic tubing, coated telephone wire;
loom woven box with long free wires included to
thread through plastic tubing and bead knot at end
Photo by Janet Charles

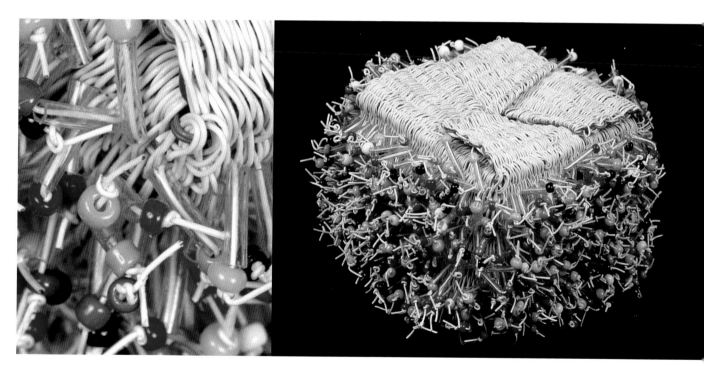

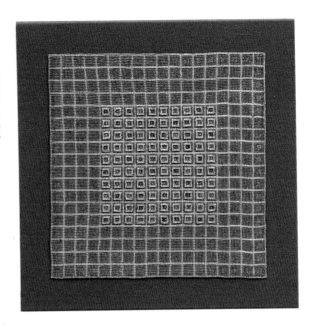

BETTY PAN
Harlequin I, 2001

16½ x 16½ x 2½ in. (41.9 x 41.9 x 6.4 cm)
Triangle beads; square stitch
Photo by D. James Dee

BETTY PAN
Harlequin IV, 2002

18½ x 18½ x 2½ in. (47 x 47 x 6.4 cm)
Triangle beads; square stitch
Photo by D. James Dee

ROBERT BURNINGHAM
Repeat Pattern Surrounded by Triangle Border, 1991

17 x 15½ in. (43.2 x 39.4 cm)
Seed beads, bugles, embroidery floss, gold thread,
H'mong indigo batik fabric; bead embroidery, embellishment
Photo by artist

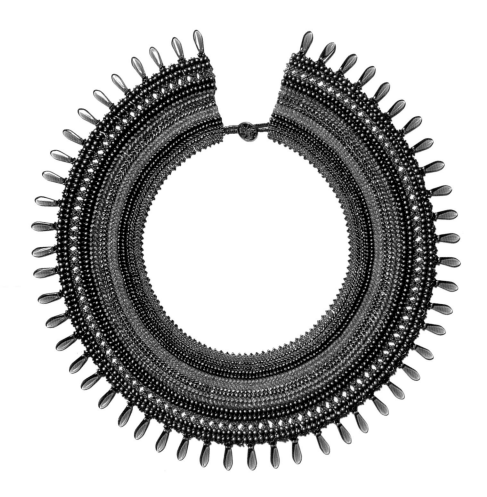

CAROLE HORN
African Sunset, 2002

3 in. (7.6 cm)
Seed beads, cylinder seed beads,
pressed glass drop beads;
herringbone stitch, netting
Photo by D. James Dee

224

NANCY KOENIGSBERG
City Lights, 2002

19 x 8 in. (48.3 x 20.3 cm)
Clear glass beads, silver-lined beads,
annealed steel wire; square-knotted
with beads incorporated in each
knot, twisted
Photo by D. James Dee
Collection of Karen and Richard Venevty

*The completed cylinder
was twisted to create a
dense spiral of sparkling
beads to suggest the
glittering movement of
city lights at night.*

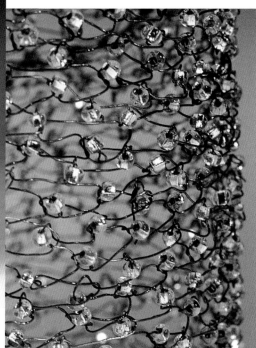

LARKIN JEAN VAN HORN
Candle Cloth, 2000

10½ in. (26.7 cm)
Seed beads, bugles, assorted beads,
cotton, candleholder by Mark Briggs;
bead embroidery
Photo by G. Armour Van Horn

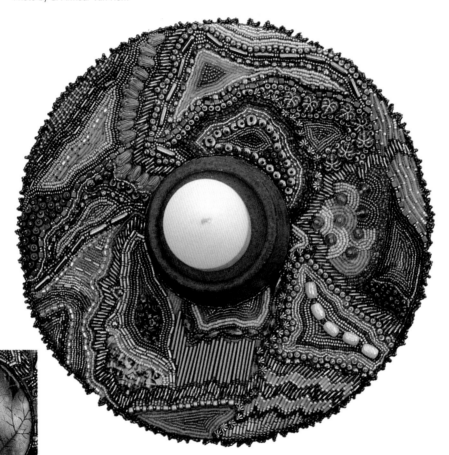

This piece was worked on a frame to ensure that it would lie flat.

DONNA L. LISH
Spectral Quake, 2003

14 x 14 x 1 in. (35.6 x 35.6 x 2.5 cm)
Seed beads; peyote stitch
Photo by artist

This mandala-like circle is the fifth in a sequence of meditative works.

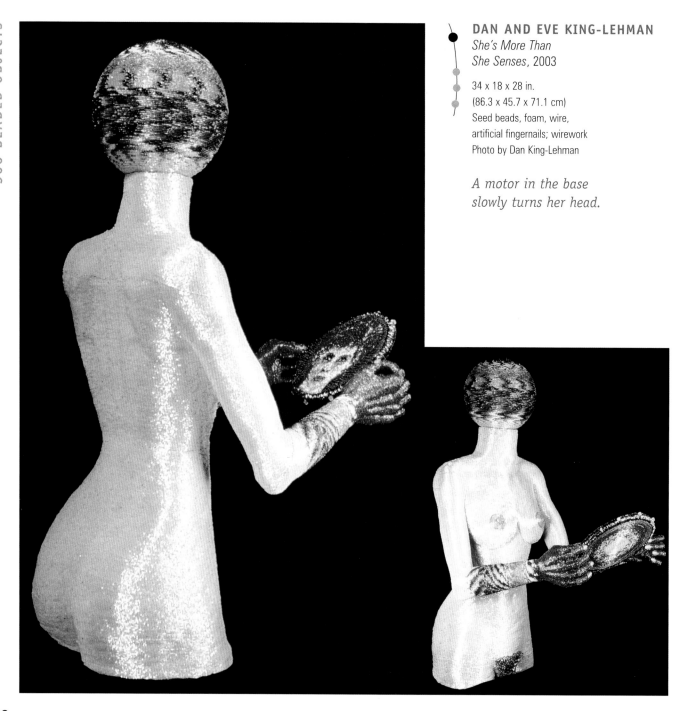

DAN AND EVE KING-LEHMAN
*She's More Than
She Senses*, 2003

34 x 18 x 28 in.
(86.3 x 45.7 x 71.1 cm)
Seed beads, foam, wire,
artificial fingernails; wirework
Photo by Dan King-Lehman

*A motor in the base
slowly turns her head.*

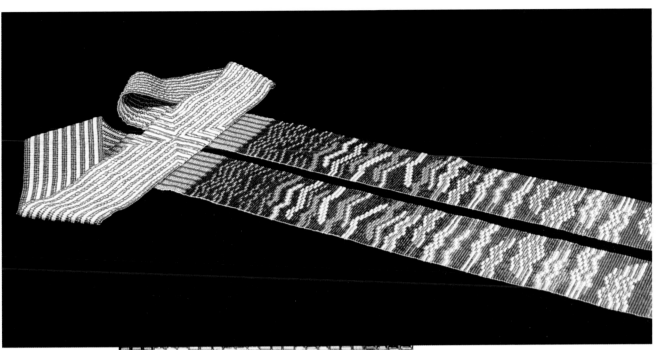

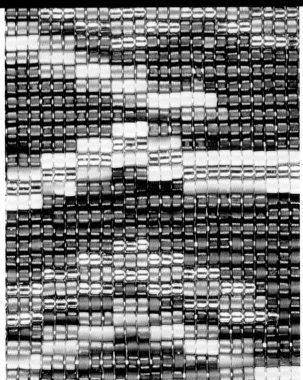

KATHERINE AMACHER KORFF
Waters of Baptism—Liturgical Stole, 2001

72 x 2½ in. (182.9 x 6.4 cm)
Glass beads; loom woven
Photo by Kathy Solar

CHRIS ALLEN-WICKLER
Jules' Journey, 1997

8½ x 5½ x 4 in. (21.6 x 14 x 10.2 cm)
Seed beads, drop beads, lake rock; peyote stitch
Photo by Peter Lee
Collection of Dana Hughes

The Visible Soul *series seeks
to identify the specific shape
and scope of a soul. Stone is a
metaphor for the soul—solid, worn,
eternal. The surface beadwork
is composed of fragile elements,
tiny increments, a cellular collection
paralleling our own delicate skins.*

230

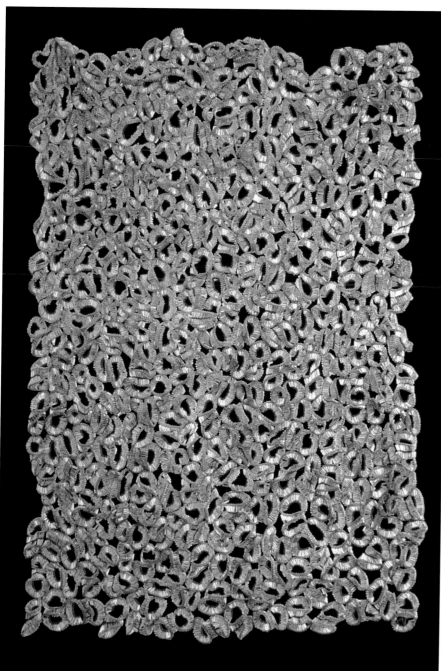

*Inspired by
the idea of a
single element
appearing as two.*

NATASHA ST. MICHAEL
Spindle, 2002

29 x 20 x 1 in.
(73.6 x 50.8 x 2.5 cm)
Cylinder seed beads,
bugles; peyote stitch
Photo by Paul Litherland
Private collection

231

SAGE ZERING
Feathered Egg, 2003

12 x 7 x 7 in. (30.5 x 17.8 x 17.8 cm)
Seed beads, assorted beads; brick stitch
Photo by Steve Talmadge

TATIANA STACY-MONTAGUE
An Essay in Elemental Magic/Fire, 2003

Front, 15 x 45 in. (38.1 x 114.3 cm);
back, 15 x 26 in. (38.1 x 66 cm)
More than 1,000 raku-fired porcelain leaf beads
made by artist, glass blade beads, seed beads,
antique brooch; leaf beads machine-sewn onto fabric,
blade beads hand-sewn, seed beads strung
Photo by Larry Sanders

*This piece is part of a larger series
that includes* Water, Earth, Air,
and Chocolate—*all essential elements
in the magic of the life process.*

233

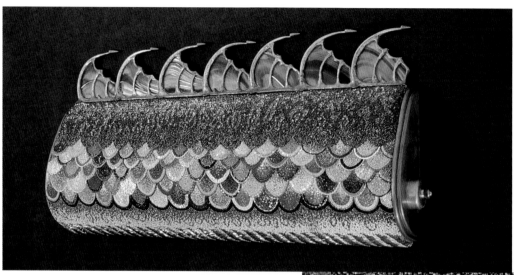

JAMES EDWARD TALBOT
The Dragon's Weak Scale, 1996

15 x 34 x 5 in. (38.1 x 86.3 x 12.7 cm)
Seed beads, stained glass, copper, brass, leather, wood, cotton; appliqué on sculptural armature
Photo by Mary Castagna

It is said that in order to slay a dragon, whether it be parental, corporate, societal, or political, you must first find its weak scale. This one is no exception.

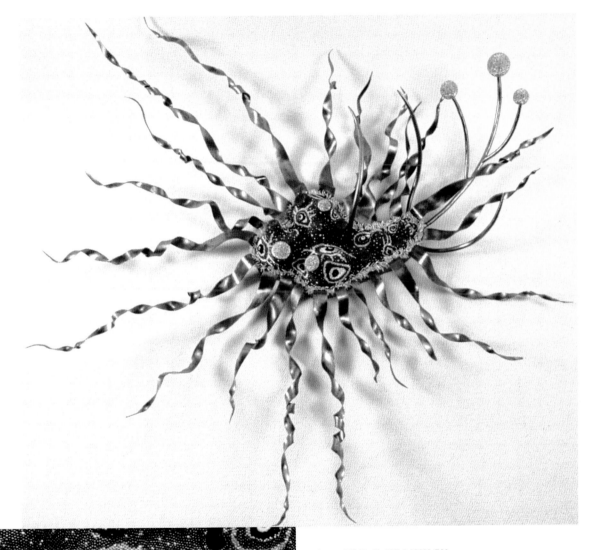

KIM Z FRANKLIN
My Dementia, 2002

48 x 54 x 12 in. (122 x 137.2 x 30.5 cm)
Seed beads, glass eyes, hand-formed clay understructure,
hand-forged metal framework by artist and Michael Franklin;
sculptural peyote stitch
Photo by Donna Chiarelli

235

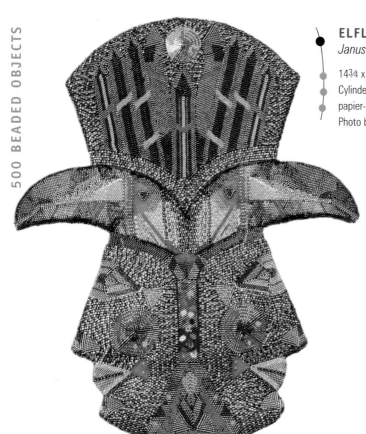

ELFLEDA RUSSELL
Janus for the Toucans, 2001

14¾ x 12¼ x 2¼ in. (37.4 x 31.1 x 5.7 cm)
Cylinder seed beads, triangle beads, plaster and
papier-mâché form; sculptural peyote stitch
Photo by artist

*This life-size mask is a tongue-in-cheek
send-up to the Roman god Janus, who is
asked to protect the dwindling habitat of the
improbable toucan.*

CONNIE LEHMAN
Tarot: XIII Death/Rebirth, 2002

7¼ x 4¾ x ¼ in. (18.4 x 12 x .6 cm)
Vintage charlottes, coral beads, vintage French sequins, silk noil;
bead embroidery, Russian needle punch (*igolochkoy*)
Photo by Roger Whitacre
Private collection

*This is one in a series of
21 major arcana tarot cards.*

KELLY BUNTIN JOHNSON
Archangel Gabriel, 2003

21 x 12 x 13 in. (53.3 x 30.5 x 33 cm)
Seed beads, brass sequins, freshwater pearls,
assorted beads, vintage fabric, leather,
brass, wood; appliqué, fringe
Photo by artist

LI RAVEN
Sergeant Pepper's Lonely Hearts Club Band, 1998

24 x 3 x 1½ in. (60.9 x 7.6 x 3.8 cm)
Seed beads, assorted glass beads;
peyote stitch, free-form stitches
Photo by K and S Studios

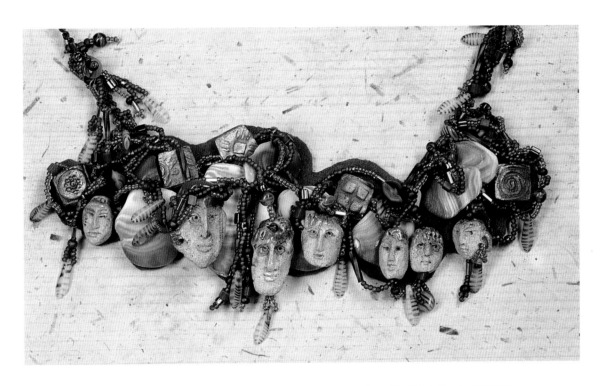

MARLA L. GASSNER
Tribe, 2000

6 x 2 in. (15.2 x 5 cm)
Found objects, suedelike fabric, handmade faces
by Fete of Clay, raku, shells, macramé
Photo by Tom Van Eynde
Collection of Wendy Warden

DAVID K. CHATT
White Men in Suits, 2002

6½ x 2 x 11 in.
(16.5 x 5 x 27.9 cm)
Assorted glass beads,
U.S. pennies;
right-angle weave
Photo by Harriet Burger

JOANN FEHER
Ethel Mermaid, 2003

2½ x 3 x 5½ in. (6.4 x 7.6 x 14 cm)
Seed beads, assorted beads, wire, wire mesh, plaster cast material,
assorted findings; three-dimensional peyote stitch, fringe, wirework
Photo by Tom Feher

TERRY PYLES
Chameleon, 2003

12 x 4 x 6 in. (30.5 x 10.2 x 15.2 cm)
Seed beads, modeling compound, wire,
glass; peyote stitch, wirework
Photo by Joe Manfredini

*This was my first beading project. It was done
entirely with peyote stitch.*

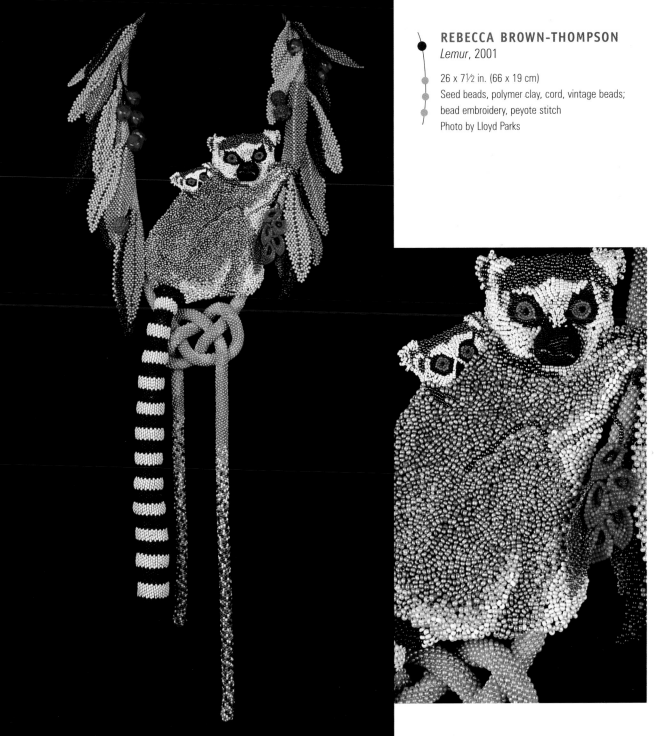

REBECCA BROWN-THOMPSON
Lemur, 2001

26 x 7½ in. (66 x 19 cm)
Seed beads, polymer clay, cord, vintage beads;
bead embroidery, peyote stitch
Photo by Lloyd Parks

SUSI JAGUDAJEV-JENKINS
Fish, 2002

4 x 6 x 2 in. (10.2 x 15.2 x 5 cm)

Seed beads, copper wire, stone beads; improvised wire weaving

Photo by Scott Parry

Collection of Kristin L. Hilfiker

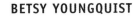

BETSY YOUNGQUIST
Fishbowl, 2002

14 x 11 x 1 in. (35.6 x 27.9 x 2.5 cm)
Seed beads, assorted beads,
vintage glass stones, acrylic ink,
watercolor board; glued
Photo by Larry Sanders

*This piece speaks about
the feeling of being watched,
examined, or judged by others.
The goldfish is out of his
element and feeling alienated.*

BETSY YOUNGQUIST
Waiting for the Rain, 2003

9 x 9 x 1 in. (22.9 x 22.9 x 2.5 cm)
Seed beads, vintage stones, acrylic ink,
watercolor board; glued
Photo by Larry Sanders

ANN TEVEPAUGH MITCHELL
Refugees, 1997

Each figure approximately 6 x 5 x 4 in. (15.2 x 12.7 x 10.2 cm)
Glass beads, stones, apothecary bottles;
peyote stitch, other stitches, assembled improvisationally
Photo by Dean Powell

CIDIAN B. SUNTRADER
Savage World, 2002

5½ x 9 in. (14 x 22.9 cm)
Seed beads, assorted glass beads, cylinder seed beads,
black glass; loom woven, peyote stitch
Photo unattributed

247

ROBIN ATKINS
Rosie, the Uncaged Hen, 2001

7 x 7 x 7 in. (17.8 x 17.8 x 17.8 cm)
Assorted vintage and new glass beads, vintage sequins, carved stone beads,
mirror, necktie label, fabric, brass armature, domed wood base; improvisational
bead embroidery worked flat in four pieces, constructed
Photo by Joe Manfredini

Rosie *evolved from improvisational bead embroidery on a
piece of cloth. As I worked on her, she came to represent
artistic freedom and playfulness.*

JOANNE STREHLE BAST
Ode to Hundertwasser, 2002

3 x 5 x 4 in. (7.6 x 12.7 x 10.2 cm) Seed beads, assorted beads,
rock with glued leather bottom; brick stitch, right-angle weave
Photo by Jerry Anthony

The colors and images are inspired by paintings by Hundertwasser.

MEGAN NOËL
Dreams and Being Dolls, 2001

6 x 2 x 2 in. (15.2 x 5 x 5 cm)
Assorted beads, suedelike fabric; bead embroidery
Photo by Jan Cook

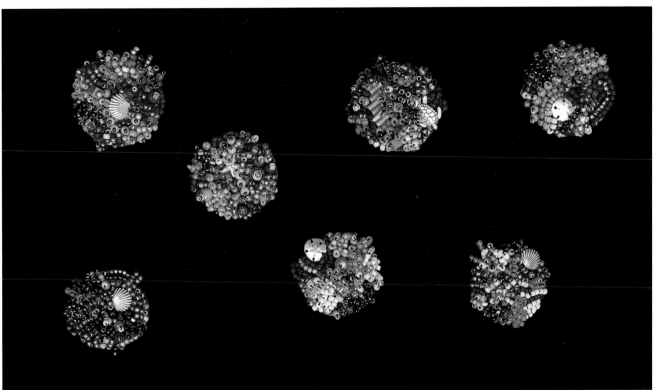

MEGAN NOËL
Beaded Coral Reef Buttons, 1998

1 in. (2.5 cm)
Seed beads, charms, fabric, metal frames;
bead embroidery
Photo by Shaun Chappell

BENEDICT J. TISA
Nana Boy, 2000

23 x 18 in. (58.4 x 45.7 cm)
Seed beads, bugles, mother-of-pearl buttons, cotton;
bead embroidery, Haitian embargo style
Photo by artist

BENEDICT J. TISA
Father's Son, 2000

19 x 16 in. (48.3 x 40.6 cm)
Seed beads, sequins, bugles, mother-of-pearl buttons,
cotton; bead embroidery, Haitian embargo style
Photo by artist

BENEDICT J. TISA
Go Slow, 2000

22 x 18 in. (55.8 x 45.7 cm)
Seed beads, sequins, bugles, old plastic buttons on cotton;
bead embroidery, Haitian embargo style
Photo by artist

BENEDICT J. TISA
Sonny Boy, 2000

19 x 13 in. (48.3 x 33 cm)
Seed beads, bugles, mother-of-pearl buttons,
cotton; bead embroidery, Haitian embargo style
Photo by artist

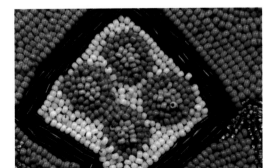

253

JEANETTE AHLGREN
Fighting Back the Gloom, 2003

13½ x 11½ x 11½ in. (34.3 x 29.2 x 29.2 cm)
Glass beads, gold wire; woven
Photo by artist
Courtesy of Mobilia Gallery

LINDA FIFIELD
Earth & Fire, 2002

18 x 7 x 7 in. (45.7 x 17.8 x 17.8 cm)
Seed beads, turned wooden vessel; gourd stitch
Photo by Jack Fifield

LINDA FIFIELD
Earth, Water, Wind & Fire, 2002

8 x 2½ x 2½ in. (20.3 x 6.4 x 6.4 cm)
Seed beads, turned wooden vessel; gourd stitch
Photo by Jack Fifield

255

CARY FRANKLIN GASPAR
Crown of Thorns Gourd, a Paradox Box, 2003

6½ x 6 x 6 in. (16.5 x 15.2 x 15.2 cm)
Seed beads, assorted beads, crystal, gourd,
sculpting compound; right-angle weave
Photo unattributed

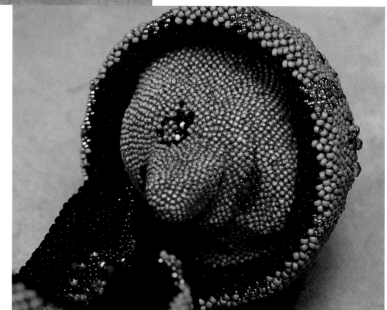

JENNIFER WHITTEN
Red Tape II, 2003

3 x 11 x 1 in. (7.6 x 27.9 x 2.5 cm)
Seed beads, ribbon, plastic tape
dispenser; loom work, assemblage
Photo by CLIX

Red Tape II *is the second in a series
called* The Bureaucrat's Desk Set.

SUSAN WOLF SWARTZ
Noli Me Tangere (Touch Me Not) II, 1995

7½ x 5 x 5 in. (19 x 12.7 x 12.7 cm)
Seed beads, bugles, accent beads,
handmade polymer clay hearts, armature;
peyote stitch, fringe, spiky fringe
Photo by Thomas Carroll

*Second in a series exploring
the relationship between the
emotions of the heart and
the rigid framework
of family structure.*

ELFLEDA RUSSELL
Raspberry Baroque, 2003

11¼ x ½ in. (28.5 x 1.3 cm)
Seed beads, triangle beads,
assorted beads, wood bead;
herringbone stitch, peyote stitch
Photo by artist

Herringbone- and peyote-stitched beads cover a wood foundation bead for the closure.

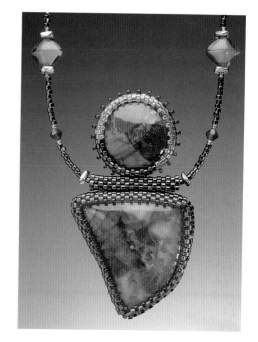

JÓH RICCI
Fall Goddess, 2000

2½ x 1½ x ¼ x 20 in. (6.4 x 3.8 x .6 x 50.8 cm)
Cylinder seed beads, porcelain cabochons, vintage
glass, Czech glass, silver- and gold-plated beads;
gourd stitch
Photo by T. R. Wailes

LINDA RICHMOND
Autumn Lariat, 2002

30 x 2 in. (76.2 x 5 cm)
Triangles, seed beads, cylinder seed beads;
herringbone stitch, peyote stitch, Russian-weave stitch
Photo by Bob Gregson

*This piece was inspired by a maple tree's fall colors,
and thoughts of Christmas approaching. I designed
hollow beaded beads to resemble Christmas ornaments.*

JAMES EDWARD TALBOT
Holy Land, 2002

53 x 30 x 2 in. (134.6 x 76.2 x 5 cm)
Seed beads, assorted beads, brass finials,
wood; loom woven, wrapped, fringe
Photo by Jeff Rowe

All *lands on the face of
this earth are holy.*

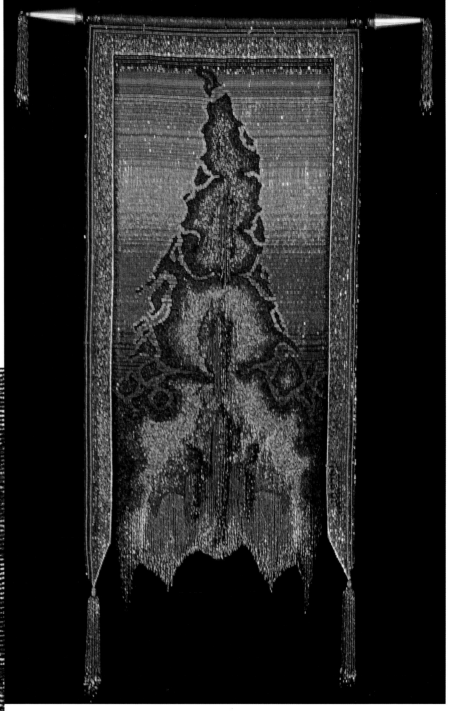

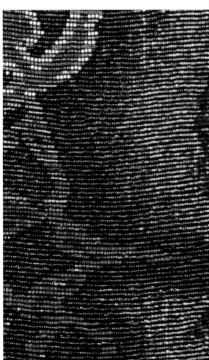

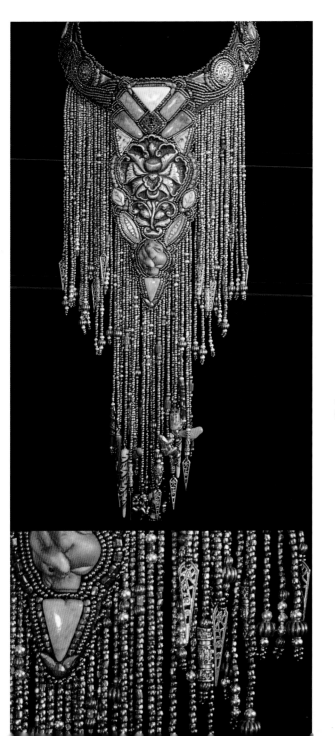

HEIDI F. KUMMLI
Forest Dance, 2003

13 x 6 x ½ in.
(33 x 15.2 x 1.3 cm)
Seed beads, sterling silver,
turquoise, carved wood;
bead embroidery
Photo by artist

DON PIERCE
Quail on the Mountain Evening Purse, 2002

8 x 6 x 1⁄2 in. (20.3 x 15.2 x 1.3 cm)
Cylinder seed beads, antique bugles, Swarovski crystals,
braided neck strap
Photo by Martin Kilmer

LAURA McCABE
Primitive Origins, 1999

12 x 91⁄2 x 2 in. (30.5 x 24.1 x 5 cm)
Seed beads, pyratized ammonites, covellite, freshwater pearls,
leather; bead embroidery, peyote stitch, embellishment
Photo by Deirdre Cunningham

This was the first large collar I made—and the
first true test of my patience and perseverance.
It took 400 hours to complete over an
eight-month period.

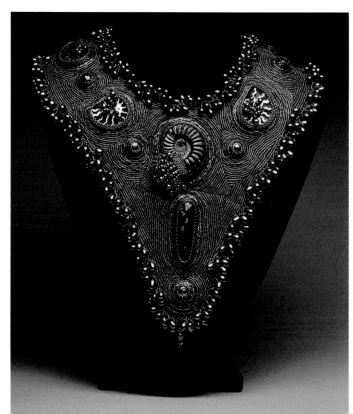

PAULA WALTER
Summer on the Vine, 2002

13 x 4½ x ⅓ in. (33 x 11.4 x .8 cm)
Seed beads, malachite, garnet, leather,
sterling silver metalwork by Lucy Ludwig,
upholstery thread; appliqué, peyote stitch,
branched fringe
Photo by Kate Cameron

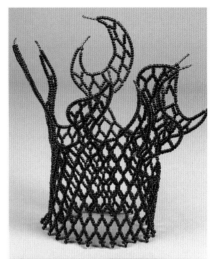

SHERRI J. THOMPSON
Litany, 1998

15 x 10 in. (38.1 x 25.4 cm)
Seed beads, assorted beads, brass button;
peyote stitch, square stitch
Photo by Larry Murphy

TERESA SULLIVAN
Flame Cuff, 2002

5 x 3 x 3 in. (12.7 x 7.6 x 7.6 cm)
Seed beads, wire; hexagonal netting
Photo by artist

264

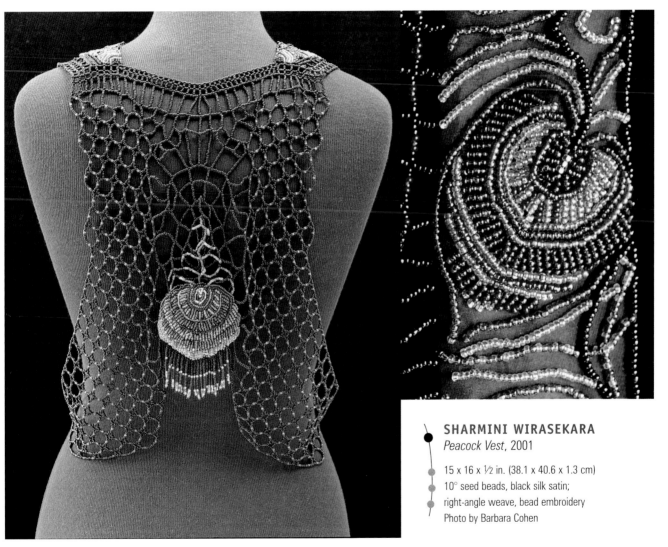

SHARMINI WIRASEKARA
Peacock Vest, 2001

15 x 16 x ½ in. (38.1 x 40.6 x 1.3 cm)
10° seed beads, black silk satin;
right-angle weave, bead embroidery
Photo by Barbara Cohen

BETSEY-ROSE WEISS
Surfacing Ideas, 1994
7½ x 3 x ½ in. (19 x 7.6 x 1.3 cm)
Seed beads, pony beads, rondelles, felt, leather;
bead embroidery, knotting, stitching
Photo by Frank Rogozienski
Collection of Marilyn Ostrow

*The necklace reflects difficult choices and
how ideas bounce and percolate inside us.
The large dimensional bubbles represent thoughts
floating randomly through energy waves:
the steely seed beads.*

CHRIS ALLEN-WICKLER
Listener, 1997

7 x 5½ x 4 in. (17.8 x 14 x 10.2 cm)
Seed beads, lake rock; peyote stitch
Photo by Peter Lee

*This was inspired by my
youngest daughter's ears
on the day she was born.*

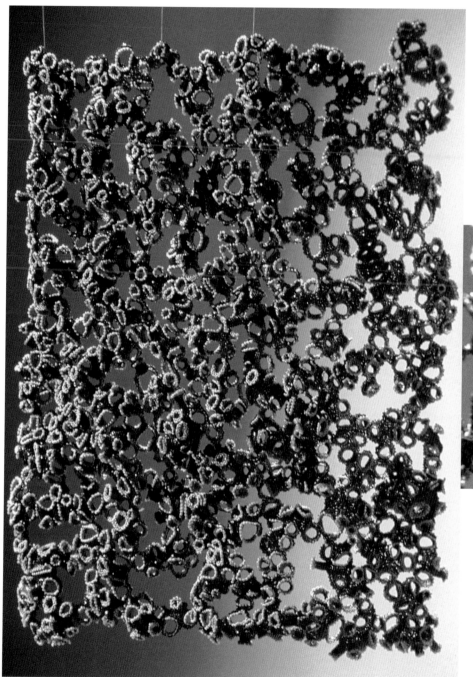

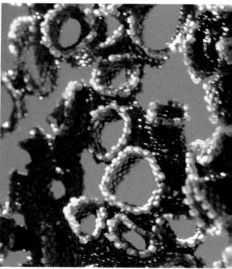

NATASHA ST. MICHAEL
Porous, 2002

20 x 18 x 1 in. (50.8 x 45.7 x 2.5 cm)
Cylinder seed beads; peyote stitch
Photo by Paul Litherland

B. J. GUDERIAN
Genie Bottle, 2003

27 x 2½ in. (68.6 x 6.4 cm)
Cylinder seed beads, fire-polish faceted beads, copper heishi
beads, assorted beads; net stitch, looped fringe
Photo by Richard Nicol

CARY FRANKLIN GASPAR
Genie of the Lamp, 2000

8 x 6 x 9½ in. (20.3 x 15.2 x 24.1 cm)
Cylinder seed beads, assorted beads, polymer clay, glass base;
right-angle weave, netting, fringe
Photo unattributed

LIZ MANFREDINI
French Maid, 1998

9 x 7 x 8 in. (22.9 x 17.8 x 20.3 cm)
Seed beads; peyote stitch, right-angle weave,
bead embroidery, fringe
Photo by Joe Manfredini
Private collection

Each bead is a 1-inch (2.5 cm) section of pencil, drilled and sharpened.

JENNIFER MAESTRE
Nuzzle, 2003

14½ x 9 x 6½ in. (36.8 x 22.9 x 16.5 cm)
Pencil stubs; peyote stitch
Photo by Dean Powell

JENNIFER MAESTRE
Messenger, 2001

18 x 9½ x 6 in. (45.7 x 24.1 x 15.2 cm)
Pencil stubs; peyote stitch
Photo by Dean Powell
Collection of Kathi Kaligian

JENNIFER MAESTRE
*Encouragement
of the Sun*, 2003

21 x 11 x 11 in.
(53.3 x 27.9 x 27.9 cm)
Pencil stubs; peyote stitch
Photo by Dean Powell
Collection of Lou Ann Daly

271

*Here is a robe
for the legendary
Snow Princess
of fairy tales.*

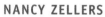

NANCY ZELLERS
Robe for a Snow Princess, 2001

14 x 11 x 4 in. (35.6 x 27.9 x 10.2 cm)
Cylinder seed beads, seed beads, Swarovski crystals, lead crystal
beads, silk satin; right-angle weave (robe base), fringe
Photo by artist

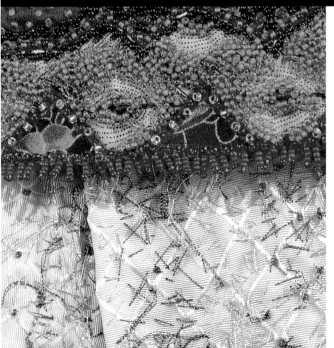

BONNIE A. BERKOWITZ
The Cloth I Am Cut From, 2000

24½ x 54 x 1½ in. (62.2 x 137.1 x 3.8 cm)
Seed beads, damask, fused cotton fabric, antique satin,
muslin, metallic threads; bead embroidery
Photo by Peter Jacobs

*Contained in each web of this
personal history book jacket are
stories and memories inscribed
with metallic threads.*

273

OLGA DVIGOUBSKY CINNAMON
Piecing Myself Back Together, 2002

9 x 4 x 2 in. (22.9 x 10.2 x 5 cm)
Various crystals, glass beads, freshwater pearls,
bone bead, fabric stuffing; crochet, free-form beadwork
Photo by Jeff Owen
Private collection

TRACY STANLEY
My How Time Flies, 2000

16 x 10 x 5½ in.
(40.6 x 25.4 x 14 cm)
Seed beads, cylinder seed beads,
accent beads, watch parts,
freshwater pearl, sterling silver wire,
copper; bead embroidery,
square stitch, peyote stitch
Photo by Joe Manfredini

275

COLLEEN O'ROURKE
Symbiotic, 2003

8½ x 6½ in. (21.6 x 16.5 cm)
Seed beads; bead embroidery
Photo by artist

Inspired by the incredible bond between mother and child.

COLLEEN O'ROURKE
Cornered, 2003

8½ x 6½ in. (21.6 x 16.5 cm)
Seed beads; bead embroidery
Photo by Colleen Jasinski

Inspired by the incredible stress brought on by having a baby.

COLLEEN O'ROURKE
Lazy Eye, 2002

9 x 15 in. (22.9 x 38.1 cm)
Seed beads; bead embroidery
Photo by artist

JUNE ARCHER MILLER
Pig Inside Out, 2000

4½ x 12 x 4½ in. (11.4 x 30.5 x 11.4 cm)

Assorted beads, spandex-covered pig form; sewn

Photo by Lynn Hunton

JUNE ARCHER MILLER
Tough Pig, 2000

4½ x 12 x 4½ in. (11.4 x 30.5 x 11.4 cm)

Assorted beads, leatherette, spandex-covered pig form; sewn

Photo by Lynn Hunton

VALORIE HARLOW
Wolfman, 2001

12 x 6 x 18 in. (30.5 x 15.2 x 45.7 cm)
Seed beads, assorted beads; peyote stitch, right-angle weave
Photo by Petronella Ytsma

The head of this piece slides open to reveal the face of a man.

279

GINI WILLIAMS
In the Midnight Hour, 2002

28 x 17 x 12 in. (71.1 x 43.2 x 30.5 cm)
Assorted glass beads, moonstones, piano wire,
oak wood, mirror, copper, metal stand,
handblown glass vase; loom woven,
peyote stitch, brick stitch, surface embellishment
Photo by Alan Miller

*This three-dimensional still life
captures a moment in time,
when a grand moth dances
above a night-blooming cereus.*

KATHY SEELY
Flutterby, 2001

11 x 10 x 6 in. (27.9 x 25.4 x 15.2 cm)
Seed beads, cylinder seed beads, fabric,
polyester fiberfill, brass wire, polymer clay;
peyote stitch and variations, bead embroidery
Photo by Robery Batey

A song on the radio gave wing to long-held emotions that had no words, and the concept for Flutterby was born.

281

DAVID J. ROIDER
Mola Alligator, 2002

6 x 4 (15.2 x 10.2 cm)
Cylinder seed beads; peyote stitch
Photo by artist

CHRISTMAS COWELL
Happy Tails to You, 2000

13 x 5½ x 1¾ in. (33 x 14 x 4.4 cm)
Seed beads, rhinestones, silver charm; Huichol technique
Photo by Chris Arend

283

JAN A. HODGES
Odalisque's Daydream, 2002

8 x 10¾ x ¼ in. (20.3 x 27.3 x .6 cm)
Seed beads, bugles, assorted beads, cotton fabric and batting;
bead embroidery, fringe, machine piecing, appliqué, stitching
Photo by Arthur E. Ryan Jr.

*This miniature hanging began as an attempt to
use up leaf-shaped leftovers from another project.
It evolved into a bead embroidery and fringe
sampler, then took on a life of its own.*

ELFLEDA RUSSELL
Samantha's Journey, 2003

10¼ x 11¼ x ⅝ in. (26 x 28.5 x 1.6 cm)
Seed beads, cylinder seed beads, two- and three-cut beads,
triangle beads, turquoise, bronze bugles, bronze novelty beads,
painted plaster foundation form; herringbone stitch, peyote
stitch, brick stitch, single-needle ladder stitch
Photo by artist

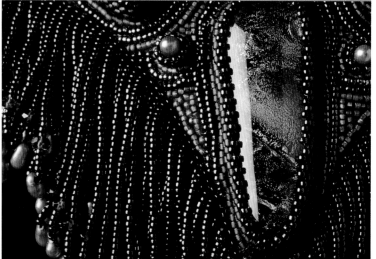

SHERRY SERAFINI
Cleveland, 2003

6 x 12 in. (15.2 x 30.5 cm)
Dichroic cabochons, seed beads,
freshwater pearls; bead embroidery,
peyote stitch
Photo by Kevin P. Ritchey

*One of the wildest
pieces I've ever done.
It feels wonderful
on the neckline and
is surprisingly light.*

SHERRY SERAFINI
Oceans of Emotions, 2002

6½ x 10 in. (16.5 x 25.4 cm)
Abalone cabochons, freshwater pearls, crystals,
seed beads, cylinder seed beads, suedelike fabric;
bead embroidery, peyote stitch, surface
embellishment, fringe
Photo by Kevin P. Ritchey

MARTA GILBERD SOSNA
Braided Bowl, 2002

5½ x 2½ in. (14 x 6.4 cm)
Seed beads, pearls, garnets,
silk cord; peyote stitch
Photo by Melinda Holden

CHARLENE ASPRAY
Peruvian Blue Opal Demi Parure, 2001

Necklace, 18½ in. (47 cm); bracelet, 7 3/4 in. (19.6 cm)
Vintage seed beads, blue opal, pearls, silver beads, silver clasp; strung
Photo by Ralph Gabriner

*This necklace and bracelet are composed of more than 650 vintage Italian seed beads
and more than 570 gemstones, pearls, and silver beads.*

RAMONA LEE
Edwardian Drawstring Purse, 2000

12 x 11 in. (30.5 x 27.9 cm)
Seed beads, pearl cotton, faceted teardrops; bead crochet, sewn
Photo by Robert Henry Sturgill

JANE FRIEDMANN
Victorian Evening Purse, 2002

8¾ x 5¾ x 1½ in. (22.2 x 14.6 x 3.8 cm)
Seed beads, triangles, glass pearls,
freshwater pearls, lampworked flower and leaf,
metal purse frame, silk; modified netting stitch,
square stitch, backstitch
Photo by Steve Schneider

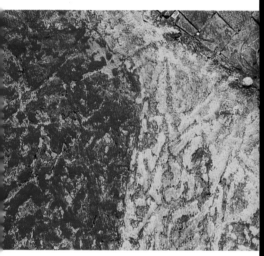

SUSAN PLANALP
Happy Days, 1992

58 x 35 in. (147.3 x 89 cm)
Seed beads, handmade abaca paper,
oil paint; loom woven
Photo by John Bonath

DONNA L. LISH
Pushing Up Daisies, 2002

12 x 7 x 8 in. (30.5 x 17.8 x 20.3 cm)
Seed beads, square beads, bugles, plastic, paint; peyote stitch
Photo by Peter Jacobs

*This house is an urn in which ashes
may be kept; a soul hospice with a
whimsical twist, embellished with designs
and details of the deceased's life.*

MIMI HOLMES
Ghost Dolly, 2002

8½ x 8 x ½ in. (21.6 x 20.3 x 1.3 cm)
Real seed beads, glass seed beads, sequins, fabric trim;
photo transfer, bead embroidery
Photo by artist

MIMI HOLMES
Mello Yello: Mummy, 2002

8 x 8½ x ½ in. (20.3 x 21.6 x 1.3 cm)
Glass and plastic beads, sequins, fabric trim;
photo transfer, bead embroidery
Photo by artist

ROBIN ATKINS
Blessings, 2003

4¹³⁄₁₆ x 5 x 1¼ in. (12.2 x 12.7 x 3.2 cm)
Assorted vintage and new glass beads, abalone cabochon, fabric, drawing paper, acrylic paint; improvisational bead embroidery, buttonhole stitch (book binding)
Photo by Joe Manfredini

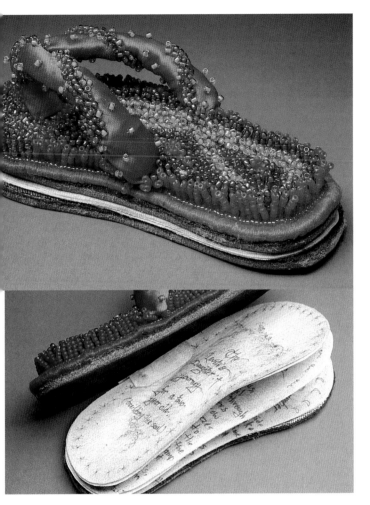

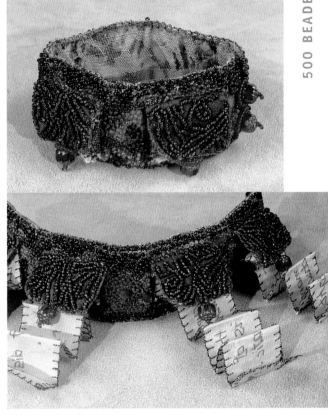

BONNIE A. BERKOWITZ
The Levite's Daughter: A Sole Book, 2000

2 x 2½ x 4 in. (5 x 6.4 x 10.2 cm)
Glass beads, leather, muslin, antique satin;
bead embroidery, fringe
Photo by Craig Phillips

*Beaded fringe stands above handwritten,
dyed muslin pages bound into the sole of
this tiny shoe, telling early childhood tales.*

BONNIE A. BERKOWITZ
Book Bracelet: Four Answers, 2000

7½ x ¾ x 2 in. (19 x 1.9 x 5 cm)
Seed beads, metallic thread, silk,
fused cotton fabric; bead embroidery
Photo by Peter Jacobs
Collection of A. Kardon

297

INGRID GOLDBLOOM BLOCH
The Source, 2003

5½ x 26 x 14 in. (14 x 66 x 35.6 cm)
Pony beads, vinyl tubing, monofilament;
peyote stitch, brick stitch
Photo by Dean Powell

*This piece is intended to capture
the beginning roots of creativity and
desire. The image of pods growing
out of tangled webs of fertile vine was
the inspiration for the forms I chose.*

BETTE KELLEY
Secret Life of Oaks, 2001

15 x 5 in. (38.1 x 12.7 cm)
Three-cut beads, bugles, seed beads,
cylinder seed beads, vintage bugles,
vintage flat-pinched, metal backbars;
picot edging, ladders, oak-leaf fringe,
overlays, braiding
Photo by Joe Van De Hatert
Model, Deshona Pepper-Robertson

*One fall, I found a leaf
of the most beautiful rose
color, with small patches of
tangerine and some brown.
When I turned it over
I realized it was an oak leaf;
its "right" side was an
unremarkable yellow with
brown and green. The beauty
lay in the secret side.
It took four tries, but I
finally achieved an oak-leaf
fringe that celebrates
"the secret side of oaks."*

SUSAN HELMER
Untitled, 2000

20 in. long (50.8 cm)
Spice beads embedded with lapis lazuli, carnelian,
and amber chips; stone doughnut spacers, leather
Photo unattributed

To make the beads I mix spices such as
cinnamon and cloves with rose water and
gum arabic. I pierce and stud them
with semiprecious chips before they dry.

CAROLINE GORE
Cut, Scrape, Incision, 1999

Beads, 1 in. diameter (2.5 cm); silk, 30 in. (76.2 cm)
Copper enameled beads, Limoges enameled beads,
copper, sterling silver, silk
Photo by artist

SHARRI MOROSHOK
Sea Anemone Necklace, 2003

22 in. (55.8 cm)
Seed beads, charlottes, cylinder seed beads;
peyote stitch
Photo by Brian McLernon

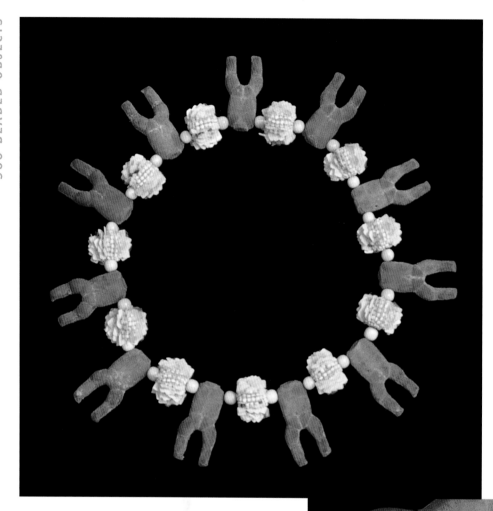

ELEANOR LUX
Little Bitty Baby Explosion, 2002

14 x 14 x 1 in. (35.6 x 35.6 x 2.5 cm)
Seed beads, latex beads, sequins; peyote stitch
Photo by Cindy Momchilou

SHARON M. DONOVAN
Baroda Necklace, 2001

1½ x 18 in. (3.8 x 45.7 cm)
Charlottes, seed beads, gold, gold wire; cast, strung
Photo by Larry Sander

MADELYN C. RICKS
Deco Rhythm, 1997

12 x 11 x ¼ in. (30.5 x 27.9 x .6 cm)
Cylinder seed beads; peyote stitch
Photo by Jerry Anthony

*This was the first piece I designed
and created after I taught myself
peyote stitch. I still think it's one of
my more successful pieces.*

DON PIERCE
Silver Pendant, 2003

2¾ x 1¼ x ¼ in. (6.9 x 3.2 x .6 cm)
Cylinder seed beads, vintage bugles, vintage cabochon,
cast sterling silver, silver cable; loom woven
Photo by Martin Kilmer

FRAN STONE
Study in Red, Gold, and Black, 2000

9 x 5 in. (22.9 x 12.7 cm)
Hex beads, vintage beads; brick stitch, peyote stitch
Photo by Melinda Holden

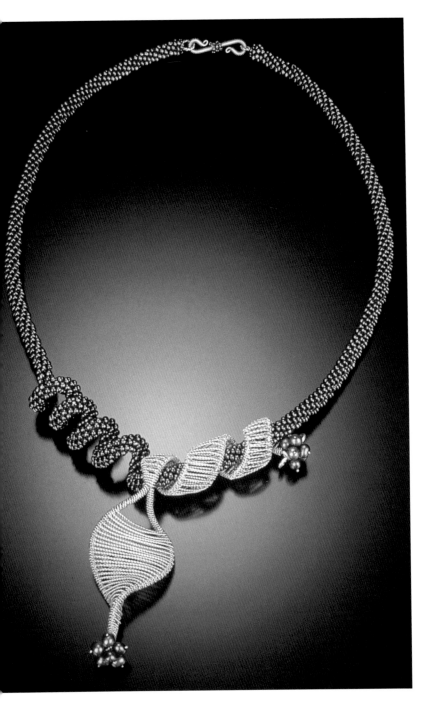

**LAUREL KUBBY AND
DALLAS LOVETT**
Autumn Leaf, 2002

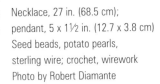

Necklace, 27 in. (68.5 cm);
pendant, 5 x 1½ in. (12.7 x 3.8 cm)
Seed beads, potato pearls,
sterling wire; crochet, wirework
Photo by Robert Diamante

DALLAS LOVETT
Ornate Treasures, 2002

4½ x 2½ in. (11.4 x 6.4 cm)
Seed beads, lampworked bead,
silver wire; wirework
Photo by Robert Diamante

VALERIE HECTOR
Golden Moon Brooch—
Parallels Series, 2002

5 x 1¾ x ½ in. (12.7 x 4.4 x 1.3 cm)
Cylinder seed beads, hex-cut metal beads,
sterling silver armature; peyote stitch tubes
Photo by Larry Sanders
Artist's collection

My Parallels *series*
brooches are inspired by
seventeenth-century
embroidered wickerwork
shields from the
Ottoman Empire.

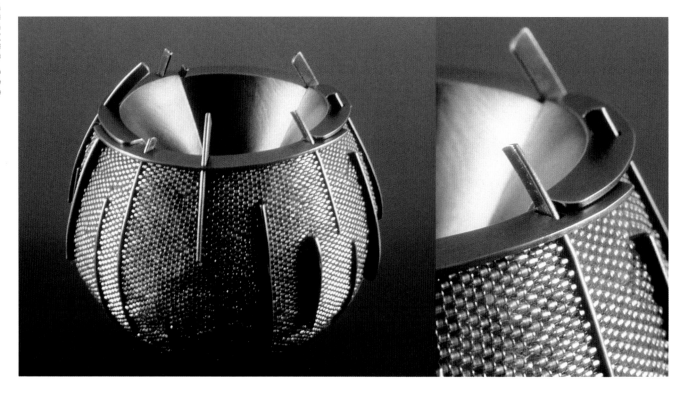

JENNIFER MOKREN
Ribbed Vessel #1, 2002

3¾ x 4 x 4 in. (9.5 x 10.2 x 10.2 cm)
Cylinder seed beads, copper; peyote stitch,
fabricated copper elements
Photo unattributed

SHARON M. DONOVAN
2.5 D Bracelet, 2001

1 x 7½ in. (2.5 x 19 cm)
Sterling silver, gold, cylinder seed beads; fabricated, woven
Photo by Larry Sanders

CAROL DE BOTH
Black and White Grass, 2000

2 x 9¼ in. (5 x 23.4 cm)
Seed beads, teardrops, safety pins,
sterling silver neck ring; right-angle weave,
peyote spikes
Photo by Tom Van Eynde
Private collection

JACQUELINE I. LILLIE
Flat Necklace, 2002

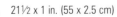

21½ x 1 in. (55 x 2.5 cm)
Antique glass beads, white gold clasp; individually knotted
Photo by Uli Kohl
Courtesy of Rosanne Raab Associates

KAREN OVINGTON
Zen, 2001

52 in. (132 cm)
Seed beads, lampworked bead,
soda glass, tassel; crochet
Photo by Tom Van Eynde

KAREN OVINGTON
Untitled, 2001

24 in. (61 cm)
Sterling silver findings, seed beads,
lampworked beads and discs; crochet
Photo by Tom Van Eynde

This piece represents my nuclear family. It was done in my son's favorite colors, silver and black. My husband's name is written in Amharic, his native language, on the bottom of the sole.

MAYRA NIEVES-BEKELE
Una Familia—un Zapato (A Family—a Shoe), 2002

10¼ x 5½ x 3¼ in. (26 x 14 x 8.2 cm)
Seed beads (glass, sterling silver, gold-plated), triangles, drop beads, hex beads, hematite hearts, onyx beads, assorted beads, moldable mesh; right-angle weave
Photo by Marty Kelly

KEN TISA
Dream, 1985

42 x 36 in. (106.7 x 91.4 cm)
Glass beads, sequins, cloth, paint
Photo unattributed

JANEENE HERCHOLD
Strutting, 2003

16 x 16 x ⅜ in. (40.6 x 40.6 x .95 cm)
Seed beads, assorted beads, pompons, gold link rings,
sequins, tied threads; surface embellishment using a
variety of bead attachment techniques
Photo by artist

*To represent movement by the bird, hand-quilted stitches with
seed beads were echoed in several layers from the body shapes.*

315

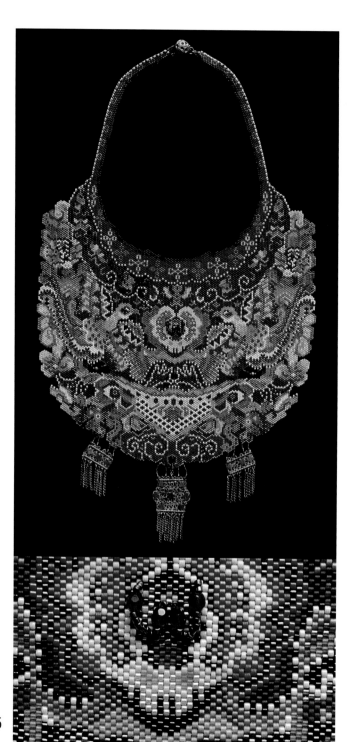

SHARMINI WIRASEKARA
Pomp and Pageantry, 2002

17 x 10 in. (43.2 x 25.4 cm)
Cylinder seed beads, crystal beads,
antique metallic ornaments; peyote stitch
Photo by Barbara Cohen

Inspired by a scarf worn at festive occasions
by the Mao women of China.

LAURA McCABE
Dahlia, 2002

27½ in. (69.9 cm)
Seed beads, moonstone,
freshwater pearls, Czech glass,
antique flower buttons;
bead embroidery, peyote stitch,
spiral weave, embellishment
Photo by Joanne Schmaltz

MADELYN C. RICKS
Kimono, 2000

10 x 10 x 1 in. (25.4 x 25.4 x 2.5 cm)
Cylinder seed beads; peyote stitch
Photo by Jerry Anthony

Kimonos are interesting to design because they have a larger flat beaded area in which to explore pattern and color.

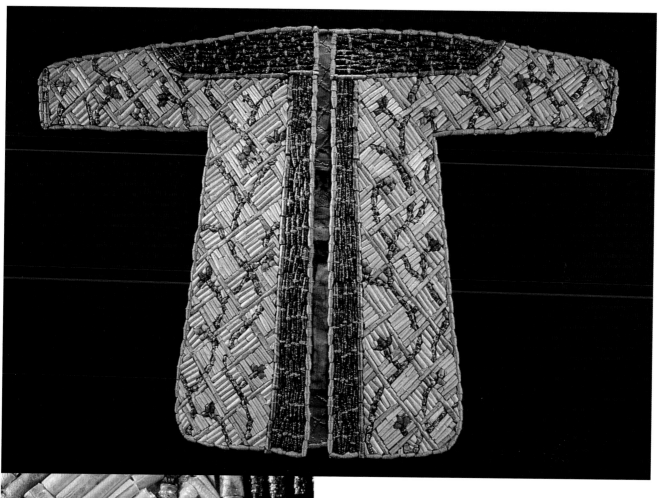

CAROLYN PRINCE BATCHELOR
St. Fiacre, 2003

12 x 17 x 1½ in. (30.5 x 43.2 x 3.8 cm)
Hand-painted paper beads, rolled individually;
sewn with metallic thread
Photo by Tom Alexander

This piece from the Garden Saints *series*
represents the garment of St. Fiacre. It opens
in front, revealing the saint's collaged image.

319

 TRACY STANLEY
She Sells Sea Shells, 1997

15 x 5 x 4 in. (38.1 x 12.7 x 10.2 cm)
Seed beads, shells, copper wire;
brick stitch, peyote stitch, fringe
Photo by Joe Manfredini

BETSEY-ROSE WEISS
Sea Blossom Necklace, 1990

6¼ x 3½ x ¼ in. (15.8 x 8.9 x .6 cm)
Seed beads, felt, leather;
bead embroidery, knotting, stitching
Photo by Frank Rogozienski
Private collection

Visiting the coast inspired this piece.
The patterns of foam outlines created by
waves hitting the sand and receding
are beautiful and fleeting.

321

KAY DOLEZAL
Collar, 2001

15 x 15 in. (38.1 x 38.1 cm)
Seed beads, teardrops; right-angle weave
Photo by Steve Gyurina

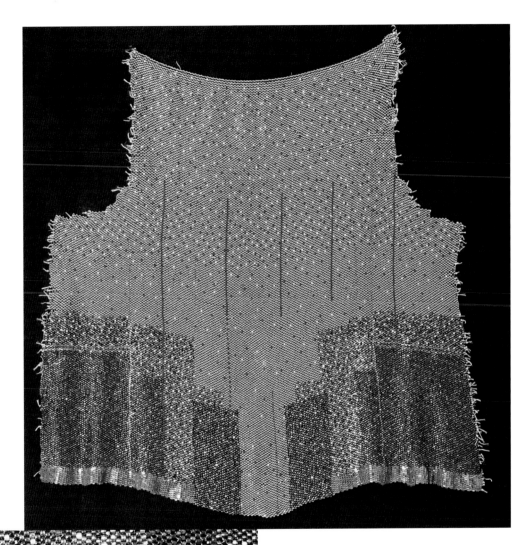

This shirt is a representation of a dream I had in which I turned into a bird. The piece took more than 2,000 hours to complete.

IRENE DORMAN
Spirit Shirt Front, 2001

15½ x 16¾ in. (39.4 x 42.5 cm)
Seed beads, assorted beads; peyote stitch
Photo by Carolyn Wright

DAVID K. CHATT
Artist in Residence, 2001

9½ x 6 x 6 in. (24.1 x 15.2 x 15.2 cm)
Assorted glass beads, wire armature;
right-angle weave
Photo by Harriet Burger

ANA M. GARCIA
Self Portrait: Silence, 2000

7 x 8 in. (17.8 x 20.3 cm)
Seed beads; right-angle weave
Photo by Melinda Holden

MARCIA LAGING CUMMINGS
Lime/Orange, 2002

12 x 7½ in. (30.5 x 19 cm)
Seed beads, resin beads, assorted beads;
peyote stitch, square stitch, brick stitch, right-angle weave
Photo by Roger Bruhn

CHRISTMAS COWELL
If the Hat Fits..., 2002

4½ x 7 in. (11.4 x 17.8 cm)
Seed beads, trade beads, lampworked bead by artist,
handmade felt, wire mesh; right-angle weave,
free-form, Ndebele stitch
Photo by Tom Edelman

*This jester's hat represents my search for something essential that
keeps me going through good times and bad. The hat actually fits me
and always brings out a smile when I put it on.*

LINDA STEVENS
Atomic Fireball Container, 2003

8 x 9 x 6 in. (20.3 x 22.9 x 15.2 cm)
Seed beads, bugles, faceted glass beads,
cylinder seed beads; glued
Photo by Mack McJunkin
Collection of Martin L. Best

TOM WEGMAN
Fish Scale, 2002

11 x 9¼ x 8 in.
(27.9 x 23.4 x 20.3 cm)
Seed beads, rhinestone chain,
vintage jewelry, vintage scale,
plastic fish; glued
Photo by David Trawick

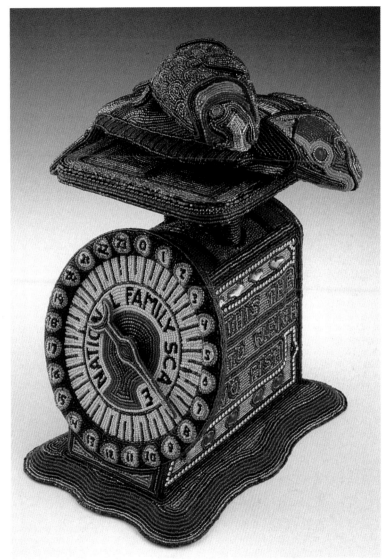

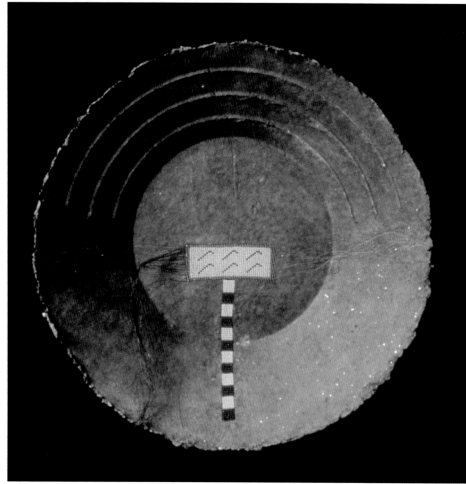

SUSAN PLANALP
Night Bowl, 1987

16 x 4 in. (40.6 x 10.2 cm)
Seed beads, cast handmade cotton paper
dyed with fiber reactive dyes; loom woven
Photo by John Bonath

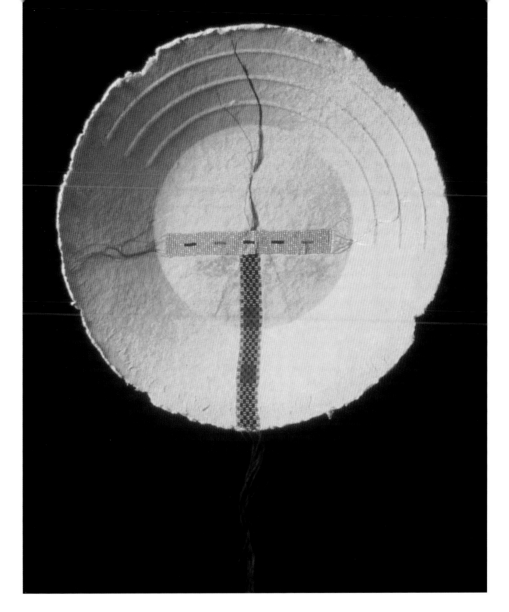

SUSAN PLANALP
Morning Bowl, 1987

16 x 4 in. (40.6 x 10.2 cm)
Seed beads, cast handmade cotton paper
dyed with fiber reactive dyes; loom woven
Photo by John Bonath

331

LINDA J. SOMLAI
360 Degrees
Unknown, 2002

65 x 49 x 2 in.
(165.1 x 124.5 x 5 cm)
Seed beads, bugles;
stitched to muslin, mounted
on gessoed canvas
Photo by Ted Wilson

*This piece,
a personal
symbol, is
meant to
connect
as a circular,
rather than a
linear, story.*

KEN TISA
She Sings, 1989

72 x 48 in. (182.9 x 122 cm)
Glass beads, sequins, paint, canvas
Photo unattributed

333

CHARLENE ASPRAY
Pearl and Labradorite Necklace, 2002

16 in. (40.6 cm)
Vintage seed beads, pearls, labradorite beads, silver clasp; strung
Photo by Ralph Gabriner

*This three-strand necklace is composed
of more than 1,400 beads.*

Inspired by looking at National Geographic *magazines as a child, my neck rings are reminiscent of those from primitive cultures. Yet the designs and structure are unique to me, as far as I know.*

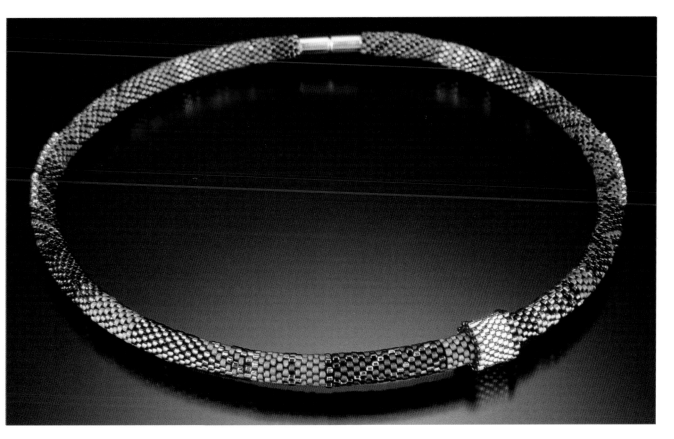

PENNY HARRELL
Autumn Phase, 2000

16 x ⅜ in. (40.6 x .95 cm)
Seed beads, sterling silver clasp; peyote stitch
Photo by Hap Sakwa

335

*The colors of the beads for this piece
simply said "coral reef." After researching
what might be found in a coral reef,
I added all sorts of organic-looking forms,
and the piece came to life.*

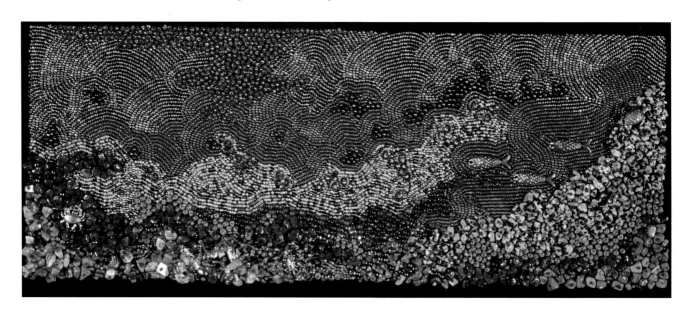

REBEKAH HODOUS
Beneath the Surface, 2002

9 x 16 x 2 in. (22.9 x 40.6 x 5 cm)
Seed beads, drop beads, gemstone chips,
pressed glass, pewter charms, cotton,
interfacing; bead embroidery
Photo by Vista Lab

MARY J. TAFOYA
La Llorona, 2002

4 x 10¼ x ¼ in. (10.2 x 26 x .6 cm)
Seed beads, charlottes, true cuts, bugles;
bead embroidery over suedelike fabric
Photo by Pat Berrett

La Llorona, *"the wailing woman," is a Hispanic folktale
of the U.S. Southwest. After killing her children, La Llorona
died and forever haunts the irrigation canals
and waterways searching for them.*

337

BETTY EDWARDS
Basket, 2000

4 x 2½ x 3 in. (10.2 x 6.4 x 7.6 cm)
Seed beads; loom woven
Photo by Sally O'Riley

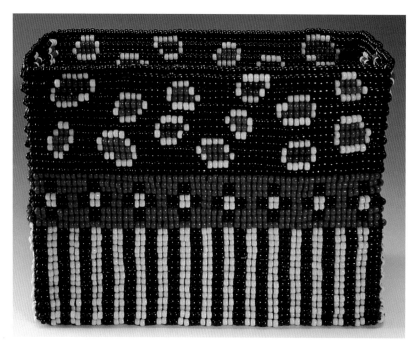

BETTY EDWARDS
Basket, 2000

4 x 2½ x 3 in. (10.2 x 6.4 x 7.6 cm)
Seed beads; loom woven
Photo by Sally O'Riley

BETTY PAN
Nested Baskets, 2000

1³⁄₈ x 1 in. (3.5 x 2.5 cm);
1 x 1 in. (2.5 x 2.5 cm);
1³⁄₄ x 1 in. (4.4 x 2.5 cm)
Cylinder seed beads; peyote stitch
Photo by D. James Dee

339

FRAN STONE
Patterns, 2003

6½ x 6 in. (16.5 x 15.2 cm)
Cylinder seed beads, drop beads;
peyote stitch, brick stitch
Photo by Melinda Holden

REBECCA PEAPPLES
Parisian Pearls, 2002

19 x 2 in. (48.3 x 5 cm)
Seed beads, cylinder seed beads, freshwater pearls;
two-drop diagonal peyote stitch, surface embellishment
Photo by Carter Sherline, Frog Prince Studios

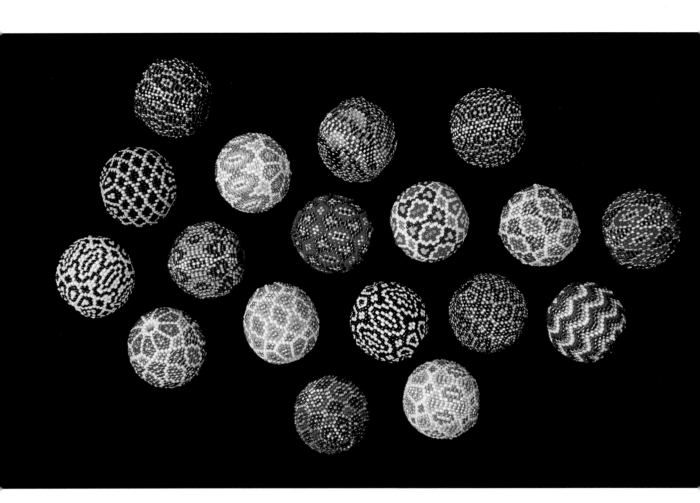

CHRISTINA MANES
Eye Candy, 2001–2003

1¼ in. diameter (3.2 cm)
Wood beads, seed beads
Photo by Edward Matuska

As a diabetic I'm not supposed to eat candy,
so I decided to make "eye candy bonbons"!

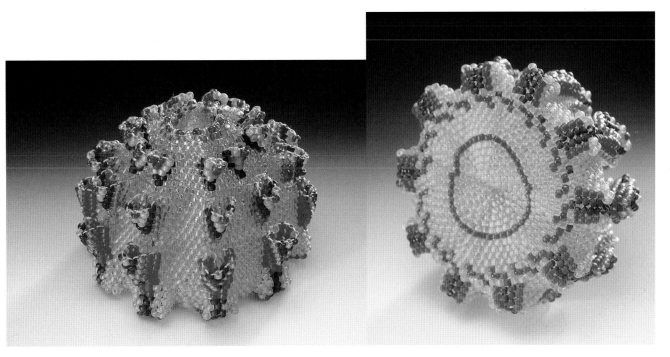

EVA S. WALSH
Bee Hive, 2001

2 x 2¼ x 2¼ in. (5 x 5.7 x 5.7 cm)
Seed beads; brick stitch
Photo by Randall Smith

BARBARA McLEAN
Party Girl, 2003

4 x 2½ x ½ in. (10.2 x 6.4 x 1.3 cm)
Seed beads, bugles, assorted beads,
porcelain face by Shannon Mayfield;
improvisational bead embroidery
Photo by artist
Collection of Sheryl Fried

BARBARA McLEAN
Polynesian Goddess, 2002

10 x 7 x 1 in. (25.4 x 17.8 x 2.5 cm)
Seed beads, miracle beads, Swarovski crystals, glass flowers, assorted beads,
porcelain face by Shannon Mayfield, lampworked leaves by Tom Simpson,
yarn hair by Laura Liska; improvisational bead embroidery
Photo by artist
Collection of Anne Coulter

BARBARA McLEAN
Poinsettia Goddess, 2001

10 x 7 x 1 in. (25.4 x 17.8 x 2.5 cm)
Seed beads, Swarovski crystals,
gold beads, assorted beads,
porcelain face by Shannon Mayfield,
lampworked leaves by Tom Simpson;
improvisational bead embroidery
Photo by artist

RACHEL LAWRENCE EDWARDS
Sole Mates, 2001–2002

8 x 15 in. (20.3 x 38.1 cm)
Opalescent beads, brass beads, discarded fabric shoes,
finishing nails, nail gun cartridges, metallic yarn, paper, ink;
stitching, crochet, airbrushing, original poems
Photo by artist

For years these shoes, given to me by a dear friend,
sat on a shelf in my studio waiting their turn.
I worked on Sole Purpose *first, then did* O Sole Mio.
Together, they're Sole Mates. *I wrote about the steps*
we take, dancing, and life in general.

KATHLYN LEIGHTON
Red-Hot, 2001

7¾ x 3½ x 10 in.
(19.6 x 8.9 x 25.4 cm)
Seed beads, bugles,
assorted sequins, two-cuts,
wire armature, molded inserts;
bead embroidery
Photo by Durk Park

Red-Hot, *also from the*
Shoe Stories *series,*
depicts my first
experiences on the
town stepping out
with one of my best
friends in school.
She was red hot.

REBECCA ROUSH
Corvus Seattlensis #2, 2001

27 x 27 x 1 in. (68.6 cm x 68.6 x 2.5 cm)
Seed beads, sequins, felt, crow feet,
pewter charm, piping; bead embroidery,
seed beads spiraled and tacked down
for body, embellishment
Photo by Joe Manfredini

*I've been working on a series of crows
specific to Seattle, Washington, since 1999.
I'm fascinated by them. Their personalities are
intricate and their relationships with other
crows rival our own human relationships.*

REBECCA ROUSH
Corvus Seattlensis #1, 2000

26 x 26 x 1 in. (66 x 66 x 2.5 cm)
Seed beads, sequins, felt, crow feet;
bead embroidery, embellishment
Photo by Joe Manfredini

The grass in this piece is made of increasingly longer (from top to bottom) strands of beads, with three strands emerging from each sequin. The sun is made of loops of beads going from sequin to overlapping sequin.

A.KIMBERLIN BLACKBURN
In Her Garden, 2002

16½ x 12½ x 10½ in.
(41.9 x 31.8 x 26.7 cm)
Carved wood, acrylic paint,
glass beads; laid in paint, some
beads strung with bead spinner
Photo by artist
Collection of Smithsonian
American Art Museum,
gift of Mitchell Bierbaum

Under the shade of the palms, she communes with her garden.

350

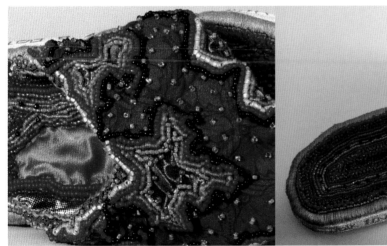

BONNIE A. BERKOWITZ
Towards a Future Path: A Life Worth Living, 2000

3 x 4 x 9 in. (7.6 x 10.2 x 22.9 cm)
Glass beads, antique satin, leather, linen, cotton fabric;
bead embroidery, couching
Photo by artist

JEANETTE AHLGREN
Divining Deceit, 2001

12 x 11½ x 11½ in. (30.5 x 29.2 x 29.2 cm)
Glass beads, oxidized brass wire; woven
Photo by artist
Courtesy of Mobilia Gallery

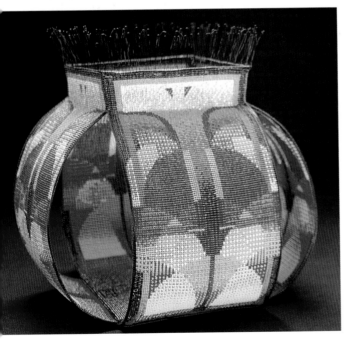

JEANETTE AHLGREN
Second Childhood, 2002

12 x 12½ x 12½ in. (30.5 x 31.8 x 31.8 cm)
Glass beads, oxidized brass wire; woven
Photo by artist
Courtesy of Mobilia Gallery

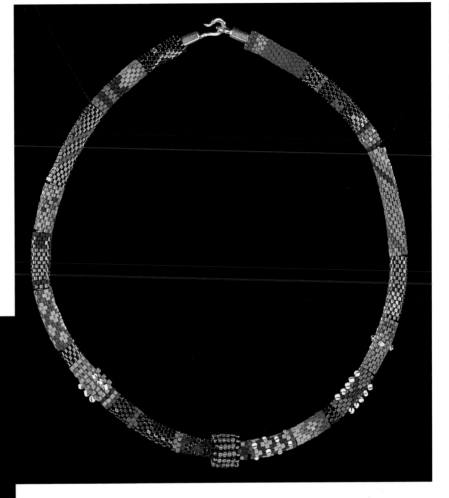

PENNY HARRELL
Beaded Neckring, 2001

16 x ⅜ in. (40.6 x .95 cm)
Seed beads, cylinder seed beads,
sterling silver clasp; peyote stitch
Photo by David Egan

353

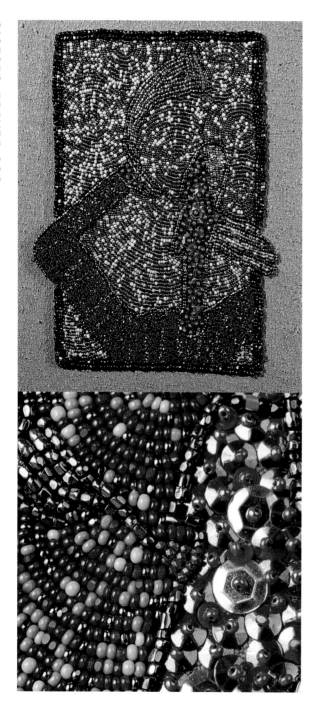

CONNIE LEHMAN
Tarot: VIII Awakening/Judgment, 2001

5¾ x 3¾ x ¼ in. (14.6 x 9.5 x .6 cm)
Seed beads, coral and turquoise seed beads,
vintage steel-cut beads, vintage French sequins,
charlottes, silk noil; bead embroidery,
Russian needle punch (*igolochkoy*)
Photo by Roger Whitacre

NAnC MEINHARDT
Diviner's Bag, 2002

10 x 13 x 1 in. (25.4 x 33 x 2.5 cm)
Seed beads, linen, interfacing; embroidered right-angle weave
Photo by Tom Van Eynde

355

KATHRYN BLACK
Green and White Snake, 1999

22½ x ¾ x ¼ (57.1 x 1.9 x .6 cm)
Seed beads, assorted beads; crochet, strung
Photo by Martha Forsyth

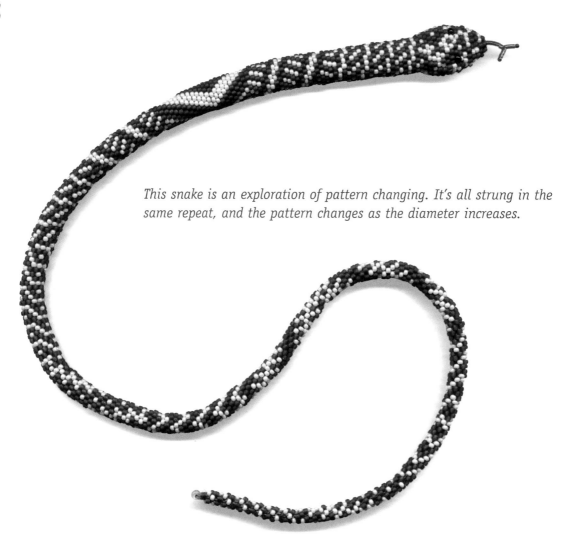

This snake is an exploration of pattern changing. It's all strung in the same repeat, and the pattern changes as the diameter increases.

RAFAEL MATIAS
Ausencia, 1998

48 x 36 in. (122 x 91.4 cm)
"E" beads, ceramic tiles,
wood; glued
Photo by Jill Conner

ROBIN ATKINS
Marriage Bag, 2000

9 x 3½ x 1¼ in. (22.9 x 8.9 x 3.2 cm)
Assorted vintage and new glass beads, charms
(abalone, brass, sterling, stone, bone), fabric;
improvisational bead embroidery, fringe
Photo by Bob Dittmer

"At age 59, shall I marry Robert?" That was the question
in my mind as I stitched beads onto cloth to make this bag.
I became increasingly warm to the idea during the 300-plus
hours it took to complete the piece. "Yes" was my answer!

KELLY SCHROEDER
Mid-Life Party!, 2002

30 x 10 in. (76.2 x 25.4 cm)
Seed beads, lampworked beads by the artist,
pressed glass beads, cane glass beads by
Dave Christensen, vintage glass beads,
copper beads, copper wire, brass rings;
sculptural wirework, strung
Photo by Azad

*I turned 40 in 2002
and decided to make a
piece celebrating the fact
that I was beginning my
mid-life party.*

THOM ATKINS
The Lotus Eater, 2003

37 x 31½ x 1½ in. (94 x 80 x 3.8 cm)
Glass beads, coral, pearls; bead embroidery, appliqué, quilting, embellishment
Photo by Tony Grant

360

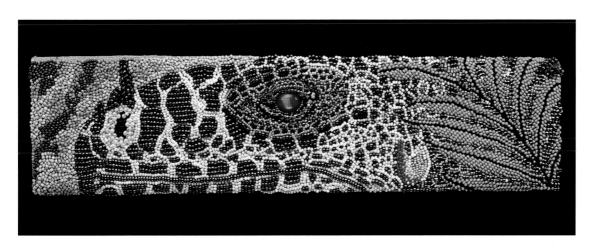

REBECCA BROWN-THOMPSON
Iguana, 2003

10 x 2½ in. (25.5 x 6.5 cm)
Seed beads, cabochon; bead embroidery,
peyote stitch, square stitch
Photo by Murray Irwin

CAROL BENNER DOELP
Japanese Iris, 2001

14 x 6 x 6 in. (35.6 x 15.2 x 15.2 cm)
Seed beads, wire; French flower beading
Photo by Kanji Takeno
Collection of John Lessner

BETTE KELLEY
I Got Them Old Turtle Blues, 1996

15 x 5 in. (38.1 x 12.7 cm)
Three-cut beads, bugles, faceted balls, seed beads,
tears, assorted dimensional beads, metal backs;
picot edging, ladders, bugle separators, three-dimensional fringe
Photo by Joe Van De Hatert
Model, Deshona Pepper-Robertson
Collection of Diane Tobias

LAURA McCABE
Conflict of Interest, 2001

14 x 10 x 2 in. (35.6 x 25.4 x 5 cm)
Seed beads, labradorite, pyritic ammonite,
rainbow obsidian, computer circuit board,
freshwater pearls, Czech glass, leather;
bead embroidery, peyote stitch, lacy stitch, branched
fringe, embellishment
Photo by Deirdre Cunningham
Photo courtesy of The Dairy Barn, Athens, OH

*The collar's front represents the oceans and
the sides represent the land. The removable back piece
represents technology and is surrounded by dead
and dying flowers, indicating the destructive effects
of technology on the natural world.*

LAURA McCABE
Sunflower Collar, 2001

15 x 12 x 2 in. (38.1 x 30.5 x 5 cm)
Seed beads, star quartz, freshwater pearls, Czech glass, leather;
bead embroidery, peyote stitch, lacy stitch, embellishment
Photo by Deirdre Cunningham
Photo courtesy of The Dairy Barn, Athens, OH

BILLIE JEAN THEIDE
Untitled, 2000

17 in. (43.2 cm)
Cylinder seed beads; peyote stitch
Photo by artist

BILLIE JEAN THEIDE
Untitled, 2000

17 in. (43.2 cm)
Cylinder seed beads; peyote stitch
Photo by artist

YOSHIE MARUBASHI
All You Need (Beader's Chatelaine), 2001

Triangle, 4 x 4 x ⅝ in. (10.2 x 10.2 x 1.6 cm);
rope, 52 in. (132 cm)
Seed beads, antique silver wax case, thread case,
thimble case, tape measure, scissors case, needle case,
snotebook; bead crochet, woven notebook
Photo by artist

B. J. GUDERIAN
Summer Honey Lariat, 2003

36 in. (91.4 cm)
Seed beads, pressed glass beads,
assorted beads; Ndebele stitch, fringe
Photo by Jerry Anthony

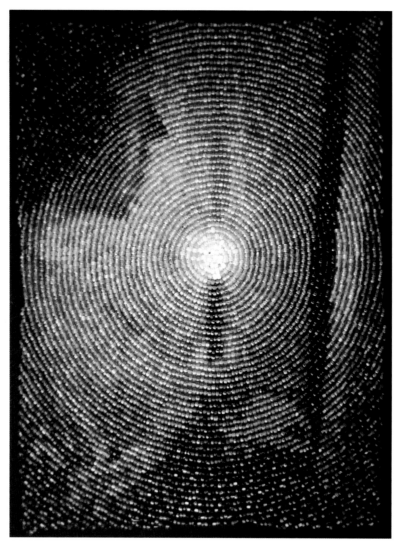

I thought about the hope inspired by the light of a single candle in darkness, and how I make a wish every time I blow out a candle.

AMY C. CLARKE
Light of Mine II: The Threshold, 2003

4 x 5½ in. (10.2 x 14 cm)
Seed beads, fabric; bead embroidery (backstitch)
Photo by artist

AMY C. CLARKE
Light of Mine III: Stairs, 2003

4 x 5¾ in. (10.2 x 14.6 cm)
Seed beads, fabric; bead embroidery (backstitch)
Photo by Reed Photo-Imaging

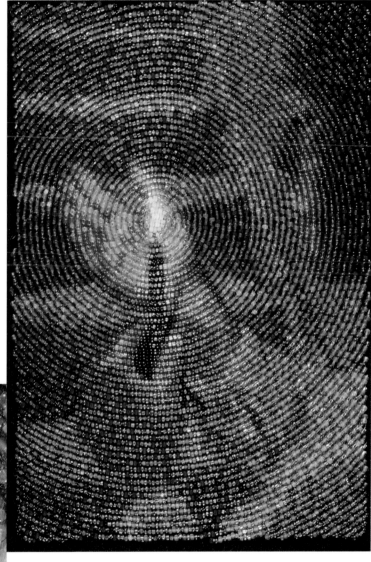

369

ROBERT BURNINGHAM
Medallion Within a Ring, 1990

14 x 14 in. (35.6 x 35.6 cm)
Seed beads, assorted beads, wool, metallic gold thread,
embroidery floss, silk floss; bead embroidery, embellishment
Photo by artist

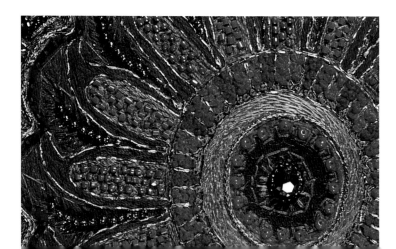

JANEENE HERCHOLD
Sunflower, 1999

22 x 22 x ¾ in. (55.8 x 55.8 x 1.9 cm)
Seed beads, sequins, pom-pons, tied threads;
machine piecing, hand-quilting, appliqué
Photo by artist

*The quilt's center is a filled shape; half with seed beads
(some sewn flat to the surface and others anchored
together for additional height) and half with tied threads
and small fabric pieces inserted for extra volume.*

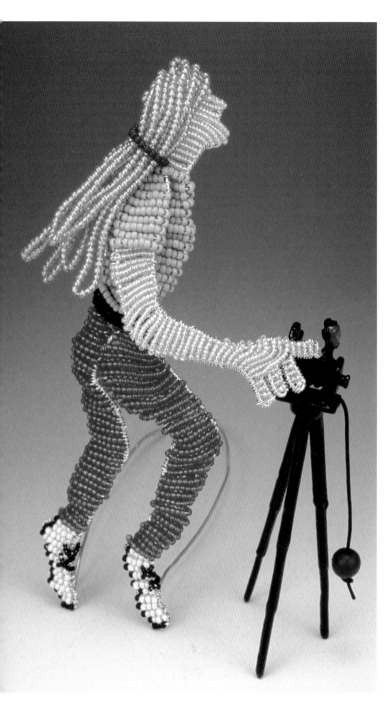

CHARLOTTE R. MILLER
You Ought to Be in Pictures, 2003

7½ x 3½ x ½ in. (19 x 8.9 x 1.3 cm)
Seed beads, miniature camera, sterling silver wire;
wirework, embellishment
Photo by Azad

DONNA L. SALETRIK
Kristen as (No, No) Nanette, 2003

6¾ x 3¾ x 3½ in. (17.1 x 9.5 x 8.9 cm)
Cylinder seed beads, assorted antique seed beads, antique bugles,
Swarovski crystals, fabric, oak box by Patches 'n Planks;
bead embroidery
Photo by David N. Saletrik

KATE ROTHRA
Caterpillar Necklace, 2002

18½ in. (47 cm)
Handblown lampworked
glass beads, composite
"coconut" beads,
Czech glass in closure
Photo by Ralph Gabriner

ELEANORE MACNISH
"Toy" Series Necklace, 2001
30 x 1½ x ¼ in. (76.2 x 3.8 x .6 cm)
Soda-lime glass beads, sterling silver wire and chain, glass beads made by artist; wirework
Photo by David Nufer
Private collection

DONNA DEANGELIS DICKT
Oriental Poppies, 2002

12 x 16 x 12 in.
(30.5 x 40.6 x 30.5 cm)
Seed beads, three-cuts;
French flower beading
Photo by artist

NORMA SHAPIRO
Patchwork Quilt Necklace, 2003

20 in. (50.8 cm)
Seed beads, lampworked beads
by artist, gold-filled cones; strung
Photo by artist

The central bead is lampworked with individual "patches" made and applied separately to the base bead. Square patch beads were strung randomly among the seed beads.

Hardware stores are treasure troves of hidden art forms. Double Take *is a study of ancient urn forms using common materials such as vinyl plumbing tubing, fishing line, and yarn.*

INGRID GOLDBLOOM BLOCH
Double Take, 2003

10½ x 6½ x 6½ in. (26.7 x 16.5 x 16.5 cm)
Quartz beads, vinyl tubing, monofilament, wool fibers; brick stitch
Photo by Dean Powell

REBECCA PEAPPLES
Brocade Collar—Silver, 2003

17 x 1 in. (43.2 x 2.5 cm)
Seed beads, cat's eye glass beads, freshwater pearls; two-drop peyote stitch, four-bead netting, surface embellishment
Photo by Carter Sherline, Frog Prince Studios

This stitch reminds me of a brocade fabric, rich and three-dimensional.

ELEYNE WILLIAMS
Saraband Collar, 2001

Outer diameter, 35 in. (89 cm); inner diameter, 14 in. (35.6 cm); widest point, 6 in. (15.2 cm)
Bugle beads, seed beads, faceted drop beads, Picasso glass, metal spacers, golden pheasant feathers; ladders, netting
Photo by Kit Williams
Private collection of Barbara Pollard

I was inspired by Egyptian broad collars and the techniques of Virginia Blakelock. This is a contemporary interpretation of an ancient form.

LUCIA ANTONELLI
Eight of Wands, 1990

22 x 5 x 3 in. (55.8 x 12.7 x 7.6 cm)
Antique Bhutanese silver
medallion, antique French brass
beads, antique silver beads,
glass beads, turquoise, coral,
leather; strung, braiding,
hand-stitching (lazy stitch)
Photo by artist

*The soothing, repetitive process of weaving each
bead to the next is by now second nature to me.
I weave the beads, off-loom, intuitively.*

SUSAN ETCOFF FRAERMAN
Bound for Glory III, 1999

5 x 9½ x 3 in. (12.7 x 24.1 x 7.6 cm)
Seed beads, freshwater pearls, semiprecious stones, found object, steel;
off-loom bead weaving, free-form right-angle weave, applied beads
Photo by Tom Van Eynde

DONNA DEANGELIS DICKT
Chrysanthemums and Hellebores, 2003

18 x 13 x 12 in. (45.7 x 33 x 30.5 cm)
Seed beads, three-cuts; French flower beading
Photo by artist

ROSEMARY TOPOL
Gardenias with Hummingbird, 2002

22½ x 12 x 9 in. (57.2 x 30.5 x 22.9 cm)
Seed beads, colored spool wire, stem wire,
floral tape, clay, florist's moss; French flower beading
Photo by Liz & Joe Schmidt Photography Inc.

MELISSA ELLIS
Aquilegia Swallowtail, 2003

16 x 12 x 12 in. (40.6 x 30.5 x 30.5 cm)
Seed beads, three-cuts,
drop beads, wire, stem wire;
French flower beading
Photo by artist

KAREN PAUST
Autumnal Equinox Necklace, 2003

9½ x 11 x 1½ in. (24.1 x 27.9 x 3.8 cm)
Seed beads, thread, wire, sterling silver;
variations on peyote stitch, needle stitch, netting
Photo by T. E. Crowley

385

A group of about 100 women from around the world who are involved in the revival of French flower beading and who are brought together through the Internet collected their spirit and energy to remember the 9/11 victims. This is one of three memorial wreaths made by the Internet's Yahoo "beadedflowers" group.

CAROL BENNER DOELP/BEADEDFLOWERS GROUP
Pentagon Memorial Wreath, 2002–2003
36 in. (91.4 cm)
Seed beads, assorted beads, wire;
French flower beading
Photo by Tod Cohen
Coordinated by Estelle Johnson

MELISSA ELLIS
Offering to Pele, 2003

20 x 12 x 12 in. (50.8 x 30.5 x 30.5 cm)
Seed beads, three-cuts, glass beads,
wire, stem wire; French flower beading,
peyote stitch, transitional netting stitch
Photo by artist

CAROL BENNER DOELP
Gold and White Orchid, 2002

15 x 8 x 5 in. (38.1 x 20.3 x 12.7 cm)
Seed beads, wire; French flower beading
Photo by Kanji Takeno

ELEYNE WILLIAMS
Colour and Weave, 2000

28 x 17 in. (71.1 x 43.2 cm)
Square-cut beads, seed beads,
bugles, bone bobbins wound
with silk and other beads,
cherry wood; loom and
off-loom woven
Photo by Kit Williams
Private collection of Brian and Janet Davis

L'MERCHIE FRAZIER
Orixa Oxumare: Joseph's Coat of Many Colors, 1996

5 x 5 in. (12.7 x 12.7 cm)
Seed beads, cylinder seed beads, sterling silver, silver and sterling silver wire, cowrie shells; bead tapestry weaving technique, sterling silver fabrication
Photo by Che Ying

L'MERCHIE FRAZIER
Xango: Shotgun House Orixa, 1996

5 x 5 in. (12.7 x 12.7 cm)
Seed beads, cylinder seed beads, sterling silver, silver and sterling wire; bead tapestry weaving technique, sterling silver fabrication
Photo by Che Ying

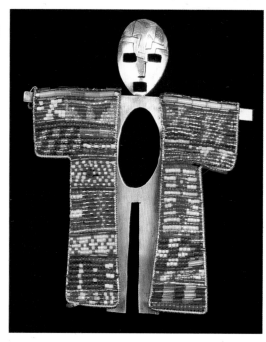

Transformation is the central theme of the Shotgun House Orixa *series, inspired by my artist residency in Brazil. I related the sacred places that house the* orixa *(deity), called* terriros, *with the shotgun houses of my home environment in the American South. The visual vocabulary of the beadwork is African and Native American.*

DENEEN MATSON
Forever Beading II, 1997

14 x 13 x 1 in. (35.6 x 33 x 2.5 cm)
Seed beads; peyote stitch
Photo by Tom Van Eynde

I've chosen to give off-loom bead weaving a unique application by creating a series of small-scale, historically based ethnic dress pieces. My ultimate responsibility is to the creators of the ethnic dress I choose to translate into beads.

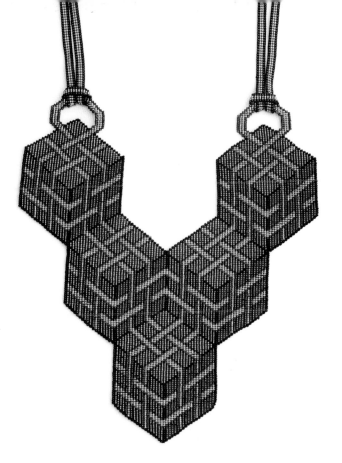

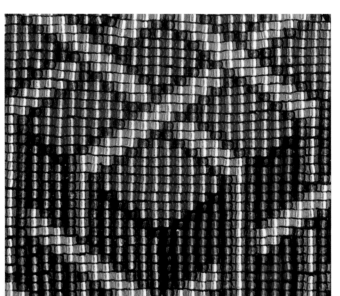

JUDY WALKER
Tumbling Blocks Necklace, 2001

9 x 7½ in. (22.9 x 19 cm)
Seed beads; loom woven, square stitch
Photo by Richard Walker

DON PIERCE
Untitled, 2002

5 x 3 in. (12.7 x 7.6 cm)
Cylinder seed beads,
antique nailheads,
Larry Scott feature
bead, silver cable;
loom woven, folded
Photo by Martin Kilmer

JENNIFER MOKREN
Ribbed Vessel #2, 2002

2¾ x 5½ x 5½ in. (6.9 x 13.9 x 13.9 cm)
Cylinder seed beads, sterling silver; peyote stitch,
fabricated silver elements
Photo unattributed

LIANE MANN
Chinese Mermaid, 2002

3 x 7 in. (7.6 x 17.8 cm)
Cylinder seed beads, brass charms, shells;
circular peyote stitch, fringe
Photo by Renée Kalmar
Collection of Maureen Kelly

LIANE MANN
Uncle Sam, 2003

3 x 6½ in. (7.6 x 16.5 cm)
Cylinder seed beads, assorted glass beads,
gold star charms; circular peyote stitch
Photo by Renée Kalmar

RONNIE LAMBROU
Carnival-A, 2002

18 in. (45.7 cm)
Seed beads, etched vintage
beads, hollow etched
lampworked beads by
Jeri Warhaftig, wire, silver
cones and clasp;
strung, wirework
Photo by Panos Lambrou

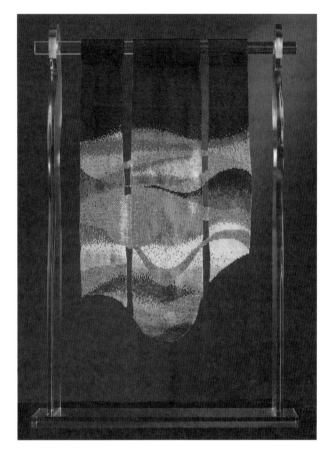

**MARGIE DEEB AND
FRIEDA BATES**
That Silver Ribbon of Road, 2003

27 x 18 x 6 in. (68.6 x 45.7 x 15.2 cm)
Seed beads (gold-plated, antique cut pewter, and glass),
acrylic stand, glass rocks; loom woven
Designed by Margie Deeb and executed by Margie Deeb
and Frieda Bates
Photo by John Haigwood

MARGIE DEEB
The Pursuit of Beauty, 1999

22 x 4 in. (55.8 x 10.2 cm)
Seed beads; split loom woven
Photo by Neil Moore

J. K. LAWSON
U.S.S. LaPlace, 2003

42 x 108 x 12 in. (106.7 x 274.3 x 30.5 cm)
Mardi Gras beads, assorted toys, preserved sailfish, plywood; glued, fabricated sail
Photo by artist
Private collection

This is a real sailfish caught in the 1960s by my client's grandfather, whose nickname was "TNT," off a pier in Bermuda. It took something like five hours to bring in. I had to remake the sail using plywood.

GINI WILLIAMS
July, 2003

22 x 5½ x ¼ in. (55.8 x 14 x .6 cm)
Glass beads, charlottes, star ruby
cabochons, antique bugles,
antique blown glass oat beads,
faceted ruby beads, freshwater pearls,
Swarovski crystal; loom woven,
peyote stitch, Russian peyote leaves,
surface embellishment, spiral rope
Photo by Alan Miller

SIOBHAN SHEEHAN-SULLIVAN
Eleanora de Toledo, 2002

6½ x 5½ in. (16.5 x 14 cm)
Seed beads, assorted beads, vintage jewelry, fabric;
bead embroidery, appliqué
Photo by artist

FRAN MENELEY
Queen Bee, 2002

15 x 5 x 2 in. (38.1 x 12.7 x 5 cm)
Seed beads, vintage sequins,
found objects, painted and
stamped linen, silk organza
Photo by Robert Morrissey

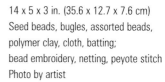

JULIA S. PRETL
Dance, 2001

14 x 5 x 3 in. (35.6 x 12.7 x 7.6 cm)
Seed beads, bugles, assorted beads,
polymer clay, cloth, batting;
bead embroidery, netting, peyote stitch
Photo by artist

*I began this piece on
September 10, 2001.
It was comforting to
work on a human form as
I watched news coverage
of so many people who
had lost their lives.*

KELLY BUNTIN JOHNSON
Our Lady of Fatima, 2001

23 x 12 x 12 in. (58.4 x 30.5 x 30.5 cm)
Seed beads, assorted beads, vintage fabrics,
leather, lace, human hair, cardboard vase,
cigar box, glass; appliqué, peyote stitch
Photo by Megan S. Wyeth
Collection of TdeP/Buntin-Johnson

Nkisi, a Kongo visual form that is believed to have the power to heal, is commonly portrayed as a human figure with a hollowed-out stomach cavity filled with secret objects. I chose to interpret Our Lady of Fatima, the Pilgrim Virgin, as revealing her secrets within.

KELLY BUNTIN JOHNSON
Our Lady of the Earth, 2003

18½ x 19 x 7½ in. (47 x 48.3 x 19 cm)
Seed beads, other glass beads,
vintage fabrics, leather, lace,
human hair, feathers, buttons;
appliqué, fringe
Photo by artist

I decided that this interpretation of the Virgin Mary would be rendered in the Cuzco school style. She would quietly remind us to protect Mother Earth.

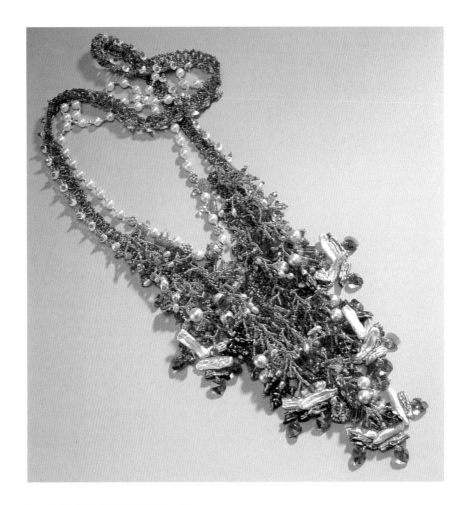

CAROL WILCOX WELLS
Chevron Elegance Necklace, 2003

19 x 4½ in. (48.3 x 11.4 cm)
Seed beads, pearls, Swarovski crystals,
rubies, assorted beads; chevron chain stitch,
spiral edging, base-braided fringe
Photo by Tim Barnwell

PAT IVERSON
Crocheted Balkan Amulet Necklace, 2001

23 x 7 x 4¼ in. (58.4 x 17.8 x 10.8 cm)
Seed beads, charlottes, three-cuts, assorted
glass beads, gold vermeil beads, gold-filled wire;
spiral crochet, sewn fringe, wirework
Photo by Martha Forsyth

*I love challenges and doing things
people tell me can't be done.*

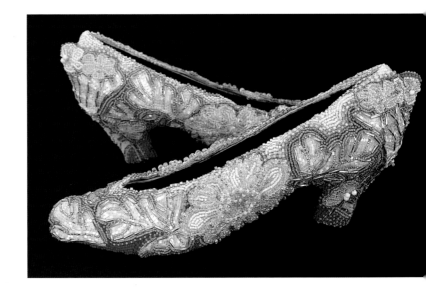

KATHLYN LEIGHTON
Cinderella Dreaming Dreams of Change, 2000

Each shoe, 4½ x 3½ x 10 in. (11.4 x 8.9 x 25.4 cm)
Seed beads, twisted bugles, two-cuts, assorted drop beads,
painted shoe inserts, lace; bead embroidery
Photo by Durk Park

Cinderella Dreaming *is one in a series of works
called* Shoe Stories, *which depicts life stories on
footwear.* Cinderella Dreaming *is a reflection
of my struggle with adolescence.*

SHEREE WILCOX
Chateau Tassel, 2003

8 x 2½ x 2½ in. (20.3 x 6.4 x 6.4 cm)
Seed beads, assorted glass beads; peyote stitch
Photo by Tom Van Eynde

FRIEDA BATES
Trellis, 1999

19 x 7 in. (48.3 x 17.8 cm)
Seed beads; loom woven, square stitch, peyote stitch, brick stitch
Photo by Mike Button

**LAUREL KUBBY
AND DALLAS LOVETT**
Copper Exploration, 2002

48 in. (122 cm)
Seed beads, potato and
heishi pearls, sterling wire;
crochet, wirework
Photo by Robert Diamante

TANYA TEGMEYER
Bohemian Rouge, 2003

Front section, 5 1/2 x 10 in. (14 x 25.4 cm)
Cylinder seed beads, pearls,
assorted semiprecious beads,
leather backing; peyote stitch,
bead embroidery, brick stitch, backstitch
Photo by John S. Green

*I made three beaded beads,
two beaded cones, and
a garnet closure for this piece,
which was inspired by the
movie* Moulin Rouge.

CAROLINE GORE
Throat, 2003

Beads, 1 in. diameter (2.5 cm); silk, 40 in. (101.6 cm)
Copper enameled beads, Limoges enameled beads,
copper, sterling silver, silk
Photo by artist

*I try to turn contemplative moments
into tangible forms.* Throat *references
a lump or knot in the throat due to
an emotional response.*

NanC MEINHARDT
9/11 Armband, 2001

7 x 6 x 7 in. (17.8 x 15.2 x 17.8 cm)
Seed beads, linen, hook-and-loop tape, interfacing;
embroidered free-form right-angle weave
Photo by Tom Van Eynde

This was my response to the 9/11 attack.

NOME F. M. MAY
Davey Jones' Necklace, 2003

12 x 8 x ¼ in. (30.5 x 20.3 x .6 cm)
Seed beads, pearls; bead embroidery, strung
Photo by Martin Kilmer

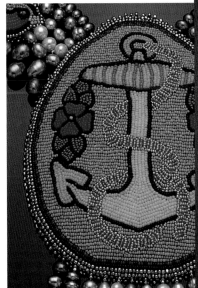

Davey Jones' Necklace *is
inspired by 1940s American
tattoo art, which adorned the
skin of hundreds of veterans.
This necklace is a tribute to
their courage and patriotism.*

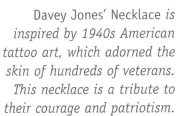

LAURA WILLITS
A Maze, 2001

17½ x 15½ in. (44.5 x 39.4 cm)
Seed beads; loom woven
Photo by Philip Arny

*Sometimes I bring a picture with me when I wake up
from a dream; this is one of them.*

412

LAURA WILLITS
Nine, 2002

12 x 18¾ in. (30.5 x 47.6 cm)
Seed beads; loom woven
Photo by Philip Arny

413

CAROL WILCOX WELLS
Dimensional Chevron Vessel and Pagoda Basket, 2001

Vessel, 9 x 4 x 4 in. (22.9 x 10.2 x 10.2 cm); basket, 3¾ x 2¼ x 2¼ in. (9.5 x 5.7 x 5.7 cm)

Seed beads, amethyst bead; dimensional chevron chain stitch, peyote stich

Photo by Tim Barnwell

LESLIE CIECHANOWSKI
Unless—(Trufula Tree), 2001

14 x 8 x 8 in. (35.6 x 20.3 x 20.3 cm)
Seed beads, foam, wire, floral tape,
bottle; right-angle weave, fringe
Photo by Joe Manfredini

*Inspired by Dr. Seuss and
the story of the Lorax.*

JENNIFER MAESTRE
Heat Wave, 2002

7½ x 5 x 4½ in. (19 x 12.7 x 11.4 cm)
Pencil stubs; peyote stitch
Photo by Dean Powell
Collection of Lynn Potoff

415

Acknowledgments

To the many hundreds of talented artists who submitted images of their beadwork from all over the world for consideration for this book, we offer our heartfelt gratitude. The range and depth of creative expression reflected by your submissions speak clearly for the medium's exciting, ongoing evolution in contemporary art.

To Carol Wilcox Wells, who honored us by taking time out from her busy schedule as a writer, teacher, and beadwork artist extraordinaire to jury the submissions for this volume. Thank you, Carol, for the careful, respectful, and fair-minded attention you gave to each of the more than 2,400 entries we asked you to review. Your patience, grace, and diligence throughout this difficult task were truly remarkable.

Thanks also to the many people at Lark Books who helped so much in making this book happen. To assistant editor Rebecca Guthrie, for her hard work and unassuming competence in handling so many details, for her help organizing the jurying process, and for her confident encouragement whenever the job at hand seemed overwhelming. To Nathalie Mornu, for her willingness to take on tasks even at the last minute. To Rosemary Kast, for typing all of those entries into our database. To computermeister Greg Evans, for giving artists access to entry information via Lark's website. To Shannon Yokeley and Lance Wille, for their invaluable art production assistance. To Rain Newcomb, for her discerning beader's eye. And certainly to art director Kristi Pfeffer, whose extraordinary sense of design speaks for itself on these pages.

Terry Krautwurst, Editor

Artists

Front Cover Artist

For nearly 20 years, **Robin Atkins**, an acclaimed bead artist who lives and works in Friday Harbor, Washington, has traveled widely teaching and researching beadwork. She has authored numerous magazine articles and four books, including *One Bead at a Time: Exploring Creativity with Bead Embroidery*. Robin writes, "I enjoy all types of beading, but especially love to sew beads on cloth. My two current passions are fabricating sculptural pieces and combining bead embroidery with bookmaking to create bead-embellished journals. I'm excited about the development of beadwork over the past two decades, as it has shifted from the world of craft into the world of art."

Contributing Artists

Jill Ackiron-Moses Woodmere, New York
Page 158

Jeanette Ahlgren Cambridge, Massachusetts
Pages 254, 352

Chris Allen-Wickler Lake Leelanau, Michigan
Pages 230, 266

Dona Anderson Burlington, Wisconsin
Page 152

Nikia Angel Albuquerque, New Mexico
Page 218

Lucia Antonelli Petaluma, California
Pages 174, 380

Charlene Aspray Los Angeles, California
Pages 289, 334

Robin Atkins Friday Harbor, Washington
Pages 248, 296, 358

Thom Atkins Santa Cruz, California
Pages 80, 360

Joanne Strehle Bast Littlestown, Pennsylvania
Pages 176, 249

Carolyn Prince Batchelor Flagstaff, Arizona
Pages 76, 319

Frieda Bates Carlsbad, New Mexico
Pages 159, 396, 407

Jo Ann Baumann Glencoe, Illinois
Pages 45, 47, 86

Dyan Bender Lafayette, California
Page 81

Barbara Berg Brooklyn, New York
Page 69

Bonnie A. Berkowitz Bloomsbury, New Jersey
Pages 55, 273, 297, 351

Kathryn Black Acton, Massachusetts
Page 356

A.Kimberlin Blackburn Kapaa, Hawaii
Pages 129, 156, 207, 350

Virginia L. Blakelock Wilsonville, Oregon
Pages 88, 114, 175

Beth Blankenship Anchorage, Alaska
Page 137

Ingrid Goldbloom Bloch Needham,
Massachusetts
Pages 298, 377

Susie Blyskal Baton Rouge, Louisiana
Page 99

Kathleen Bolan Trenton, Michigan
Page 184

Rebecca Brown-Thompson Cashmere,
Christchurch, New Zealand
Pages 162, 243, 361

Virginia Brubaker Chicago, Illinois
Pages 19, 194

Karen Bruner Pasadena, California
Page 188

Robert Burningham St. Paul, Minnesota
Pages 108-109, 223, 370

Jean Campbell Eden Prairie, Minnesota
Page 12

David K. Chatt Seattle, Washington
Pages 17, 104, 240, 324

Pat Chiovarie Seattle, Washington
Pages 95, 177

Leslie Ciechanowski Seattle, Washington
Pages 163, 415

Olga Dvigoubsky Cinnamon Upland, California
Pages 66, 274

Ann Citron Alexandria, Virginia
Page 85

Sonya Y. S. Clark Madison, Wisconsin
Pages 17, 34-35

Amy C. Clarke Lakewood, Colorado
Pages 196-197, 368-369

Diann M. Cottrill Miamitown, Ohio
Page 22

Christmas Cowell Anchorage, Alaska
Pages 283, 327

Leland Jay Crow Oxford, Ohio
Page 135

SaraBeth Cullinan Waddell, Arizona
Page 157

Marcia Laging Cummings Lincoln, Nebraska
Pages 103, 148, 326

Norris Dalton Fayetteville, Arkansas
Page 185

Carol De Both Oak Park, Illinois
Pages 220, 310

Margie Deeb Roswell, Georgia
Pages 159, 396

Suzanne Dickerson Odessa, Texas
Page 41

Donna DeAngelis Dickt Oak Hill, Virginia
Pages 204, 375, 382

Carol Benner Doelp Baltimore, Maryland
Pages 362, 386, 387

Kay Dolezal Waltham, Massachusetts
Pages 218, 322

Sharon M. Donovan Ann Arbor, Michigan
Pages 10, 11, 143, 303, 309

Irene Dorman Santa Fe, New Mexico
Page 323

Betty Edwards Madison, Wisconsin
Page 338

Rachel Lawrence Edwards Canyon Lake, Texas
Page 346

Nancy Eha Stillwater, Minnesota
Page 115

Melissa Ellis Vernonia, Oregon
Pages 384, 387

Wendy Ellsworth Quakertown, Pennsylvania
Pages 44, 83, 131, 208

JoAnn Feher Seattle, Washington
Page 241

Margo C. Field Albuquerque, New Mexico
Pages 40, 200

Linda Fifield McKee, Kentucky
Pages 37, 255

Diane Fitzgerald Minneapolis, Minnesota
Page 166

Karen Flowers Phoenix, Arizona
Page 90

Wendy Ford Coralville, Iowa
Page 80

Martha Forsyth West Newton, Massachusetts
Pages 141, 216

Susan Etcoff Fraerman Highland Park, Illinois
Pages 23, 89, 381

Kim Z Franklin West Chester, Pennsylvania
Pages 73, 235

L'Merchie Frazier Jamaica Plain, Massachusetts
Page 389

Jane Friedmann Minneapolis, Minnesota
Page 291

Jennifer Gallagher Silverton, Oregon
Page 64

Jill Gandolfi Danville, California
Page 138

Ana M. Garcia Chula Vista, California
Pages 38, 325

Cary Franklin Gaspar Woodstock, Illinois
Pages 140, 256, 268

Marla L. Gassner Phoenix, Arizona
Pages 90, 91, 239

Joe Girtner Brea, California
Page 136

Nancy Goldberg Tallahassee, Florida
Page 201

Suzanne Golden New York, New York
Pages 212-213

Ina Golub Mountainside, New Jersey
Page 139

Caroline Gore Interlochen, Michigan
Pages 301, 410

B.J. Guderian Colville, Washington
Pages 268, 367

Valorie Harlow Chanhassen, Minnesota
Pages 53, 122, 127, 279

Penny Harrell Laguna Beach, California
Pages 60, 335, 353

Lauren Harvey Chicago, Illinois
Page 172

Valerie Hector Wilmette, Illinois
Pages 20, 307

Susan Helmer Newark, California
Page 300

Janeene Herchold San Diego, California
Pages 315, 371

Mary Hicklin San Diego, California
Page 146

Susan Hillyer Washougal, Washington
Page 183

Jan A. Hodges Williamsburg, Virginia
Page 284

Rebekah Hodous Cleveland, Ohio
Page 336

Mimi Holmes Minneapolis, Minnesota
Pages 195, 294-295

Carole Horn New York, New York
Page 224

Pat Iverson Somerville, Massachusetts
Page 405

Sandra Jaech Issaquah, Washington
Page 165

Susi Jagudajev-Jenkins Portland, Oregon
Pages 126, 244

Dori Jamieson Traverse City, Michigan
Pages 98, 215

Jacqueline Johnson Yonkers, New York
Pages 107, 149, 153, 170

Kelly Buntin Johnson Dearborn, Missouri
Pages 237, 402-403

Mary H. Karg Loveland, Ohio
Page 67

Marcia Katz Jensen Beach, Florida
Page 167

Bette Kelley Yellow Springs, Ohio
Pages 75, 299, 363

Dan & Eve King-Lehman Somis, California
Pages 84, 228

Nancy Koenigsberg New York, New York
Pages 39, 147, 221, 225

Katherine Amacher Korff Fort Gratiot, Michigan
Page 229

Al Krueger Waukegan, Illinois
Pages 18, 130

Laurel Kubby Phoenix, Arizona
Pages 150, 306, 408

Heidi F. Kummli Nederland, Colorado
Pages 77, 180, 261

Gillian Lamb Woking, Surrey, England
Page 169

Ronnie Lambrou West Orange, New Jersey
Pages 211, 395

J.K. Lawson New Orleans, Louisiana
Pages 128, 397

Ramona Lee Port Hadlock, Washington
Page 290

Connie Lehman Elizabeth, Colorado
Pages 116, 236, 354

Kathlyn Leighton Bellevue, Washington
Pages 51-52, 347, 406

Laura Leonard Minneapolis, Minnesota
Pages 120-121, 122

Sally Lewis Tampa, Florida
Page 125

Jacqueline I. Lillie Vienna, Austria
Pages 32, 46, 142, 311

Donna L. Lish Clinton, New Jersey
Pages 155, 227, 293

Dallas Lovett Phoenix, Arizona
Pages 145, 150, 306, 307, 408

Eleanor Lux Eureka Springs, Arkansas
Pages 16, 171, 302

Eleanore Macnish Albuquerque, New Mexico
Pages 47, 141, 374

Jennifer Maestre Concord, Massachusetts
Pages 270-271, 415

Christina Manes Rapid City, South Dakota
Pages 124, 342

Liz Manfredini Shoreline, Washington
Pages 164, 187, 269

Liane Mann Victoria, British Columbia, Canada
Page 394

Sherry Markovitz Seattle, Washington
Pages 25, 118

Collis Caroline Marshall Louisville, Kentucky
Page 193

Christine Martell Hillsboro, Oregon
Page 82

Celia Martin Walla Walla, Washington
Page 119

Yoshie Marubashi New York, New York
Pages 48, 367

Rafael Matias Los Angeles, California
Pages 111, 357

Deneen Matson Highland Park, Illinois
Pages 71, 390

Nome F. M. May Eugene, Oregon
Pages 188, 411

Laura McCabe Noank, Connecticut
Pages 262, 317, 364-365

Ruth M. McCorrison Boulder, Colorado
Page 160

Joanne McFarland Smithfield, Virginia
Page 209

Barbara L. McGonagle Oxford, Ohio
Page 135

Barbara McLean St. Paul, Minnesota
Pages 344-345

NanC Meinhardt Highland Park, Illinois
Pages 59, 190, 355, 410

Fran Meneley Niwot, Colorado
Pages 31, 400

Charlotte R. Miller Studio City, California
Pages 13, 129, 372

June Archer Miller Foster City, California
Page 278

Leslie Milton Ridgewood, New Jersey
Page 106

Ann Tevepaugh Mitchell Wayland,
Massachusetts
Pages 13, 123, 154, 191, 246

Jennifer Mokren Green Bay, Wisconsin
Pages 33, 134, 308, 393

Sharri Moroshok Tallahassee, Florida
Pages 217, 301

Mayra Nieves-Bekele Oakland, California
Page 313

Martha C. Nikla Sarasota, Florida
Page 219

Megan Noël Seattle, Washington
Pages 250-251

Christine Marie Noguere Marble Hill, Georgia
Pages 33, 105

Colleen O'Rourke Grand Rapids, Michigan
Pages 186, 276-277

Karen Ovington Chicago, Illinois
Page 312

Betty Pan New Rochelle, New York
Pages 134, 222, 339

Paula Ann Parmenter San Marcos, California
Pages 96-97, 173

Karen Paust York, Pennsylvania
Pages 87, 202-203, 385

Rebecca Peapples Ann Arbor, Michigan
Pages 341, 378

Carol Perrenoud Wilsonville, Oregon
Pages 65, 164

Huib Petersen San Francisco, California
Page 43

Chris Ann Philips Northlake, Illinois
Pages 14, 79

Don Pierce Coos Bay, Oregon
Pages 74, 262, 305, 392

Susan Planalp Astoria, Oregon
Pages 292, 330-331

Julia S. Pretl Baltimore, Maryland
Page 401

Terry Pyles Ketchikan, Alaska
Pages 8, 242

Li Raven Evanston, Illinois
Page 238

Adele Recklies Brooklyn, New York
Page 58

Jóh Ricci New Oxford, Pennsylvania
Pages 61, 105, 259

Linda Richmond Sandpoint, Idaho
Page 259

Madelyn C. Ricks Naples, Florida
Pages 57, 128, 304, 318

Angela Riehl Lafayette, Louisiana
Page 172

Michelle Riley Paonia, Colorado
Page 182

Katherine Robinson Powder Springs, Georgia
Page 103

Robinsunne Rockport, Maine
Pages 26-27

David J. Roider Mount Kisco, New York
Pages 157, 282

Maggie Roschyk Gold Canyon, Arizona
Pages 101-102, 149

Kate Rothra Charleston, South Carolina
Pages 46, 210, 374

Rebecca Roush Seattle, Washington
Pages 112, 348-349

Elizabeth W. Rusnell Roswell, New Mexico
Page 91

Elfleda Russell Vancouver, British Columbia,
Canada
Pages 192, 236, 258, 285

Axel Russmeyer Hamburg, Germany
Page 46

Donna L. Saletrik Amherst, Ohio
Page 373

Shantasa Saling Sun City, California
Page 179

Judy Saye-Willis Faribault, Minnesota
Page 169

Kelly Schroeder Aurora, Colorado
Page 359

Scott Schuldt Seattle, Washington
Pages 62-63

Wendy Seaward Knoxville, Tennessee
Page 15

Kathy Seely Oliver Springs, Tennessee
Pages 36, 42, 281

Sherry Serafini Natrona Heights, Pennsylvania
Pages 178, 286-287

Norma Shapiro Wirtz, Virginia
Pages 61, 376

Siobhan Sheehan-Sullivan Centerport,
New York
Pages 119, 399

Sally Shore Locust Valley, New York
Page 151

Debra Smith Anchorage, Alaska
Page 184

Linda J. Somlai Racine, Wisconsin
Pages 110, 332

Marta Gilberd Sosna San Diego, California
Page 288

Natasha St. Michael Montreal, Quebec,
Canada
Pages 144,145, 231, 267

Tatiana Stacy-Montague Olympia, Washington
Page 233

Tracy Stanley Kirkland, Washington
Pages 275, 320

Andrea L. Stern Chauncey, Ohio
Page 131

Linda Stevens Abbeville, South Carolina
Pages 133, 328

Fran Stone Portland, Oregon
Pages 305, 340

Marcie Stone San Diego, California
Pages 44, 92

Carol Straus Austin, Texas
Page 100

Teresa Sullivan Portland, Oregon
Page 264

Cidian B. Suntrader Sacramento, California
Page 247

Susan Wolf Swartz Highland Park, Illinois
Page 257

Mary J. Tafoya Albuquerque, New Mexico
Pages 113, 189, 337

James Edward Talbot Austin, Texas
Pages 28, 234, 260

Tanya Tegmeyer Indianapolis, Indiana
Page 409

Billie Jean Theide Champaign, Illinois
Pages 214, 366

Sherri J. Thompson Seattle, Washington
Pages 98, 264

Benedict J. Tisa Washington, DC
Pages 252-253

Ken Tisa New York, New York
Pages 111, 314, 333

Rosemary Topol Lynbrook, New York
Page 383

Larkin Jean Van Horn Freeland, Washington
Page 226

Judy Walker Monrovia, California
Pages 9, 391

Eva S. Walsh Winter Park, Florida
Pages 115, 343

Paula Walter Mariposa, California
Pages 79, 93, 263

Dustin Wedekind Fort Collins, Colorado
Pages 49, 50

Tom Wegman Iowa City, Iowa
Pages 21, 48, 132, 329

Betsey-Rose Weiss Asheville, North Carolina
Pages 74, 266, 321

Carol Wilcox Wells Asheville, North Carolina
Pages 10, 404, 414

Jennifer Whitten Cleveland, Ohio
Pages 68, 257

Sheree Wilcox Oakland, California
Pages 72, 406

Eleyne Williams Horsley, Glocester, England
Pages 70, 94, 379, 388

Gini Williams Hendersonville, North Carolina
Pages 173, 280, 398

Michelle Williams Wilmette, Illinois
Page 24

Laura Willits Seattle, Washington
Pages 198-199, 412-413

Sharmini Wirasekara West Vancouver, British
Columbia, Canada
Pages 71, 78, 265, 316

Jo Wood Hovland, Minnesota
Pages 56, 87, 161, 205

Lea Worcester Eden Prairie, Minnesota
Page 20

Cindy Wrobel St. Louis, Missouri
Pages 29, 30, 54, 168

Betsy Youngquist Rockford, Illinois
Pages 117, 194, 245

Donna Zaidenberg Long Grove, Illinois
Pages 32, 181

Nancy Zellers Aurora, Colorado
Pages 104, 272

Sage Zering Richmond, California
Pages 206, 232

Jan Zicarelli Excelsior, Minnesota
Page 57